VISUAL THINKING STRATEGIES FOR INDIVIDUALS WITH AUTISM SPECTRUM DISORDERS

VISUAL THINKING STRATEGIES FOR INDIVIDUALS WITH AUTISM SPECTRUM DISORDERS –

The Language of Pictures

Ellyn Lucas Arwood, Ed.D.
Carole Kaulitz, M.Ed.
Mabel Brown, M.A.

APC

P.O. Box 23173
Shawnee Mission, Kansas 66283-0173
www.asperger.net

© 2009 Autism Asperger Publishing Co.
P.O. Box 23173
Shawnee Mission, Kansas 66283-0173
www.asperger.net

Publisher's Cataloging-in-Publication

Arwood, Ellyn Lucas.

    Visual thinking strategies for individuals with autism spectrum disorders : the language of pictures / Ellyn Lucas Arwood, Carole Kaulitz, Mabel Brown. -- 1st ed. -- Shawnee Mission, Kan. : Autism Asperger Pub. Co., c2009.

        p. ; cm.

        ISBN: 978-1-934575-50-5
        LCCN: 2009929576
        Includes bibliographical references and index.

        1. Autistic children--Education. 2. Asperger's syndrome--Patients--Education. 3. Visual learning. 4. Metacognition in children. 5. Teachers of children with disabilities--Handbooks, manuals, etc. I. Kaulitz, Carole. II. Brown, Mabel. III. Title. IV. Title: Language of pictures.

LC4717.8 .A79 2009
371.94--dc22   0907

This book is designed in Warnock Pro and Immi.

Printed in the United States of America.

Dedication

In consideration of the time we took from our families to work with our many students and clients over the years, we would like to dedicate this book to our children –

Sarah, David, Robert, and Elizabeth.

Your moms!

TABLE OF CONTENTS

Acknowledgments

We would like to thank our families and friends for their help with this project. Specifically, we would like to thank Tom, Ellyn's husband, for the extraordinary time and effort he put into making the figures ready for publication. As Carole says, "He is magic!" We also want to thank Jordan Ackerson, Heather Carvalho, Jan Downing, Nikki Ekle, Brenda Hiegel, Lyn Larfield, Kitty Mulkey, Nicki Roggenkamp, Bonnie Robb, and Alyse Rostamizadeh for their contributions of materials, drawings, and/or case studies. We have tried to maintain specific student and client confidentiality while also recognizing the individual professionals' contributions; so, in some cases, we have not put your name with your actual contribution. In places where there is no student or client identification associated with your contribution, we have credited you. In any case, we truly are grateful and want to say "thank you" for allowing us to include your contribution in this book.

And, to the many authors and illustrators who granted us permission to use their visuals, we say thank you for your collegiality in granting us permission. We appreciate all that you do in the profession to reach individuals diagnosed with autism spectrum disorders, and we appreciate working with you.

We would not have been able to complete this book if it were not for the many parents and families who have entrusted their children to us for therapy over the years. Furthermore, many of our students' families granted permission for us to use materials from their sons and daughters. Thank you for allowing us to use those materials so we can share what we do with other professionals and their clients' and students' families!

– Ellyn, Carole, and Mabel

Preface

Ian, a 9-year-old male, who is diagnosed with autism, sits rocking back and forth in the corner of a medical waiting room. Suddenly, he jumps up and picks up a TV Guide. He opens the booklet and turns to a page. Ian stares at the page and then climbs up on a chair to change the television channel. It is obvious that even though he does not talk, cannot use sign language, and cannot read, Ian knows what the patterns of the words on a page mean. And, from looking at these patterns, he can turn the television to one of his favorite shows.

How can a child, like Ian *think* in the print on a page without oral language and without knowing the alphabetic properties of letters and sounds for reading and writing? *The Language of Pictures* is about how a person is able to *think* through his *vision*, not through the sound of words or speech.

A Vision of Thinking

The Language of Pictures tells a story about how to use visual graphics, illustrations, photographs, cartoons, and/or flowcharts to meet the learning needs of individuals who think using visual metacognition. Visual metacognition is a means of thinking. It is the way a person makes visual sense out of the world. For example, Ian is able to *see* the meaning of the print on the page because he *mentally sees* ideas that represent the print, and he does not hear the sounds of the words when he looks at the print. Print is a form of pictures. And, thinking in a vision of print is the basis for Ian's language of pictures. So, if a child like Ian looks at print and creates a mental vision, then the mental vision becomes the basis for his language. For Ian, print was used to name the picture while the adult formed manual signs in Ian's hands as language for the picture of the print. In this way, Ian immediately began to sign the meaning of the pictures. *For Ian, the print created a vision of thinking with the language of pictures.*

Vision Thinking Through Pictures

There are many ways to think about the use of pictures as a way to create meaning. The most common thinking is that pictures can be seen and are therefore "visuals." However, just because a person is shown a picture, it does not mean that the picture holds meaning for the person looking at it. For example, a variety of visuals had been used with Ian. Educators had tried to teach him sign language, but he did not learn to use them for anything other than a response to a prompt. His parents had tried to teach Ian the names of letters so he could write his name, and he had not learned the alphabet or how to write his name. Speech pathologists had tried to use symbolic pictures (e.g., Bondy, 2001) in a communication book and as part of a picture exchange communication program; but, Ian never used the book for his communication.

For Ian, none of these "visuals" had the meaning of language. Ian just kept growing into a bigger child; and, therefore, was more difficult to handle. A special educator worked with Ian's behavior, but the training had not generalized to any setting outside the discrete trial setting. Typical work with sounds, pictures, and behavior had not worked. He could not make sufficient meaning from the looks of the letters and sounds, from the pictures, or from the visual models of behavior. Ian could physically see, but he could not mentally make a vision of thinking from what he saw. The lack of effectiveness of these different therapies and treatments is in part because all visuals are not the same. Just because something is "visual" does not mean that a person can make language from the visual so as to be able to think about the visual. Table P.1 shows some of the most common uses of the word "visual."

Table P.1

Common Uses of the Word "Visual"

Visual Term	Meaning	Educational Purpose	Educational Implication
Visual style	Educated preference or belief of how one learns	Personal preference for teaching materials. *Example:* I highlight everything in my textbook … obviously highlighting is not helping the person learning what is important.	Visual style or visual learner may not match thinking or learning system
Visual modality	Input-output method	Used for teaching. *Example:* The teacher uses all words on a PowerPoint so students can see the words, but most do not learn what the words mean until they go home and make their own mental pictures.	Visual modality is external, not internal
Visual materials	Something that can be seen and is used for education or learning	If a material can be seen, it is considered visual. *Example:* A communication board is used with a child, but the child never uses the board for his own communication.	Seeing is not necessarily "knowing"
Visual learning system	How a human being neurobiologically learns concepts that language represents	Visual-perceptual or motor-perceptual patterns overlap to form concepts for thinking. *Example:* Most children with ASD are able to create the shapes of words as bubbles, which make mental concepts (more in later chapters).	Internal "knowing" is language based

Visual Term	Meaning	Educational Purpose	Educational Implication
Visual discrimination	Acuity	Measure of what eyes physically do. *Example:* Medical doctors check to be sure the eyes function properly, but glasses do not make a person understand what he or she can see.	Seeing isn't knowing
Visual perception	Recognition of internal sensory input	Meaning is limited to recognition of patterns. *Example:* A child might copy the words on a page, which means he can recognize the patterns, but he still may not understand what the concepts for the pattern imitation mean.	Can replicate, imitate, regurgitate, fill-in-the blank, model, practice pattern, develop skills; but perception is not "knowing"
Visual concepts	Mentally thinking in graphic forms, such as pictures, movies, rolodex of words, print	Learning of concepts represents the way a person thinks … visual concepts occur through the overlap of visual and motor patterns. *Example:* A child is able to look at print on a page, "cat," and mentally see a vision of his real cat in his head; these visions are concepts.	Input for learning matches the way the person forms concepts for maximum thinking and learning
Visual language	Technology uses this term, but so does education; visual languages are contextual and relational	Understanding that the characteristics of a visual language match the concept formation of a visual thinker. *Example:* Chinese is a visual language; it uses the visions of how ideas relate as opposed to the sound of words like English, which is an auditory language based on the sound of the word.	Thinking occurs in the way that visual languages function
Viconic language™[1]	Imposing visual language functions onto auditory English language characteristics	Translating auditory culture into visual thinking. *Example:* Arwood creates techniques like talking with words that make mental pictures so as to use the properties of a visual language to help a person think in the vision of language pictures.	Provides a student with a visual way of thinking that matches with strategies for learning in an auditory world

From the contents of Table P.1, it is critical to realize that the word "visual" is used in many different ways; sometimes as a way to represent the modality, sometimes a preference or style, and sometimes as the way the learning system acquires concepts. Because the use of the word "visual" means so many different concepts, there is not much clarity in the field on when and how to use "visuals" like pictures to create sufficient meaning for education purposes.

Some people mistakenly think that as long as a child can physically see, the child will be able to create meaning for anything that is put in front of her eyes. The same adults believe that all visuals are the

---

[1] This term was coined by Ellyn Arwood and should be referenced when used. Trademark has been applied for.

same. That is, if an educator or parent shows a child a picture, the assumption is that the child is able to see the meaning of the picture as a mental vision of thinking.

Unfortunately, this is not the case. A child must be able to attach the thinking that goes with the visual in order to have sufficient meaning to develop language. For example, Ian at the beginning of the book had to have the print attached to the picture and the shape of the sign in his hand to be able to create the thinking that goes with the pictures. Otherwise, he did not see the meaning of the picture. Likewise, letters by themselves were meaningless. He needed to see the meaning of the shape of a word that represented a mental concept to know the language for the idea.

The Language of Pictures will provide many examples of how to make "visuals" a meaningful way to think in the language of pictures. The authors will provide strategies for how to understand the meaning of using "visuals" such as pictures or graphics to make language for educational purposes.

Note: The authors are not referring to learning styles. Learning styles refer to "preferences" for how material is received, not the way a person thinks. This book discusses how to think in visuals. Language then represents the thinking.

Language of Pictures

The Language of Pictures refers to the conceptual meaning a person has for visuals. This meaning originates partly with the language of the creator of the pictures; but more often, the meaning originates with the person interpreting the meaning of pictures. One person creates a picture; another person interprets what the picture means. In the communicative act of creating and interpreting pictures, each participant brings a level of language, a level of social development, and a level of cognitive development to the picture or visual. All materials, graphics, and pictures possess language: The person creating the visual uses his or her personal Language of Pictures while the person looking at the visual also uses his or her own personal Language of Pictures to understand the meaning of the visual.

Since the creator of a visual may be functioning at a different developmental level than the person interpreting the picture or visual, there may be a misperception or even misconception between what the creator of the picture meant and what the interpreter of the picture understood. That is, the picture possesses not only the creator's meaning but also the level of meaning of the person who is interpreting it. This book will help the reader understand how to match the developmental levels of pictures and visuals to the developmental level of the person looking at the visual to achieve effective use and understanding of visuals. In this way, appropriate visuals provide the language development for children with autism spectrum disorders.

Today, visual graphics and materials, once difficult to find, are commonplace. Educators, support specialists, and parents say they use "visuals" or "graphics" to help children and adults learn, especially those diagnosed with autism spectrum disorders (ASD), who think using a visual learning system (e.g., see Arwood, 1991; Arwood & Kaulitz, 2007; Grandin, 1992, 1995). However, not all people find that they are successful in using visuals to help individuals with ASD. And, when not successful, a common reaction is to increase the time working with the visuals or to stop using them. However, the problem with the intervention may not be with the visuals but with the type of visuals used. ***For visuals to be effective, the language level of the pictures or graphics must match with the language level of the child or adult who is interpreting the visuals.*** This book will help the reader determine what the developmental language level is for visual materials, including pictures, and will help the reader learn why the developmental level of visuals, as well as the developmental level of the learner, are so important in intervention.

The majority of today's school population uses a visual way of thinking and, therefore, along with those diagnosed with ASD, also need developmentally appropriate visuals to effectively learn (Arwood, 1991; Arwood & Kaakinen, 2004). Even the media have caught on to drawing their commercials with stick figures to explain a complex oral message. For example, United Parcel Service uses a dry-erase board and a brown marker to draw stick figures to explain their services. The assumption is that the listener is an astute observer, capable of reading more information from the visuals than gained from the spoken words. In reality, pictures provide an endless array of meaning for observers to interpret. For example, two different people may look at the same picture and interpret entirely different ideas.

One person might look at the picture drawing above and say that the drawing is about a trip to Alaska while another person might say the picture drawing is about the pilgrims at Plymouth Rock. Pictures are not conventional forms. Therefore, they can mean an endless array of ideas to the people who are looking at them. But, when a person draws or creates an *original* picture, that picture represents the person's own level of language, social, and cognitive development. The emphasis here is on "original," because pictures can be copied or replicated without much meaning. However, when a person draws a picture, the originator or creator of the picture brings a certain level of language, social, and cognitive development to the making of the picture or visual. This book will help the reader ascertain how visuals represent the developmental levels of learners for assessment and intervention purposes. Visuals can provide the language of thinking when the visuals are used at an appropriate level in the way that a child learns concepts best.

Using the Language of Pictures to Help Children Learn to Think

Educators, parents, and support specialists can use knowledge of developmental levels to determine the language, social, and cognitive level of a person who creates visuals. ***The person who creates visuals functions at an independent language, social, and cognitive level from the person who interprets*** *the created visual*. This book will help the reader see how to make visuals fit to a learner's developmental needs in terms of language, social, and cognitive development. In this way, the developmental level of the visual or picture matches the developmental level of the learner. By knowing a child's language level, pictures can be used to help the child learn to think, socially and cognitively.

All pictures tell a language story. And, all learners represent their language, social, and cognitive developmental levels when either creating a visual or interpreting a visual. This book will use lots of examples of various visuals such as pictures to demonstrate the various developmental levels of the visuals as well as intervention purposes for having the learner use visuals. In this way, a person's production of visuals can be a form of assessment and an educator's use of educational materials can assist a learner's social, cognitive, and/or language development. Examples of students' use of visuals will also be provided to help tell the story of the Language of Pictures.

Since all educational materials have a language, social, and cognitive developmental level, it is prudent to use materials that match the learners' levels of development. For example, using a picture that is a single object such as a ball seems to be the simplest type of picture. This is true for the adult who has complex and sufficient language to fill in the empty card with meaning related to the object so as to recognize the picture of a "ball." But, for a child with limited language, this type of picture is actually more difficult than a picture that shows how a person throws an object like a ball when outside in the park. This book will explain how the complexity of pictures or visuals is influenced by language, the language level of the child, as well as the language level of the educator or parent working with the child.

The rationale behind explaining the Language of Pictures is to help provide developmentally appropriate material for all learners. The theory behind the language, social, and cognitive levels comes from Arwood's Neurosemantic Theory of Language Learning (Arwood, 1983, 1991; Arwood & Kaulitz, 2007), which holds that learning is a socio-cognitive process of acquiring language through four meaningful stages: Sensory Input, Perceptual Pattern Development, Concept Development, and Language Development. Language represents a person's conceptual development (cognition) and the assigned meaning (socialization) from others in the person's culture (e.g., Lucas, 1980). Since the theory is explained elsewhere in the literature, this book will weave the theory into the story of the Language of Pictures for a more applied emphasis.

The authors have used a variety of visuals for more than 80 years of combined professional work. Through our careers we have learned to be very specific about what types of materials to use and what form the visuals should take. We often meet professionals who indicate that they have tried "drawing," "cartooning," or other pictorial representations but have not had the success they wanted. Throughout this book, we emphasize that *the success of using visuals is greatly dependent on matching the visuals with the language, social, and cognitive levels of the learner*. Thus, assessing the way a person learns and his language, social, and cognitive development is important for planning effective intervention.

For example, one of the authors used real-time drawings of cartooned stick figures to explain rules to a 10-year-old, such as what he looked like when he walked down the hall and what he looked like when he stood in line in the cafeteria. This process of drawing stick figures in real time worked well for the student. When the author drew the stick figures, the child watched her hand and developed his own "vision of thinking." A teacher in the school saw the child responding well to the stick figures so she decided that if stick figures worked, photographs would be that much better. So she spent a week taking photographs of the child engaged in many different daily activities.

But when she used the photographs with the child, they were not effective. Because both the stick figures (drawn in real time) and the photographs were "visuals," this educator decided that the stick figures had been a fluke and not only abandoned the photographs but quit trying to use visuals at all. She went back to rewarding the child for his behavior with tangible reinforcement. The child got bigger, but he did not develop his thinking.

What this teacher did not understand was that, developmentally, the photographs were a lot more complex than the two-dimensional stick figure cartoon, drawn in real time. Because this 10-year-old had limited social language, the stick figure cartoon was easier for him to understand than the photographs.

Another 10-year-old who talks a lot but has difficulty with more abstract concepts may also find a two-dimensional drawing of a concept easier to retrieve than a photograph of a concept, because the drawing is specific to the child's conceptual understanding. These differences in developmental needs are based on the students' learning systems as well as their social, cognitive, and language levels. Matching their learning systems to the developmental levels of materials is partially based on how the eye and brain connect to form mental concepts and how the meanings of concepts connect to the brain through language.

Summary

Educators, parents, and especially scholars, must strive to clarify the meaning of "visuals" used in education. What a person sees with the eye is different from what a person recognizes as meaningful. Knowing what a volcano is differs from the ability to recognize the written visual word "volcano." Saying the word "volcano" is different from knowing what a volcano is. Knowing is thinking, and thinking is conceptual. Vision thinking is conceptual. Concepts can be visual mental graphic forms. Concepts are systems of perceptions or recognized patterns that interconnect to form new meanings. Language represents the thinking of the concepts. So, one person could see, recognize, know, think, and/or represent ideas in a visual way. Similarly, another person could see, recognize, know, think, and/or represent ideas with different visuals.

Pictures are not just visuals but are representations of the language of the thinker who uses the picture for meaning. The emphasis in this book will be on how to select "visuals" based on how people learn social and cognitive concepts to provide visual thinkers with visual language through Viconic language™ strategies. Readers will be provided the rationale for the interconnection between learning of mental concepts and the development of language. *The Language of Pictures* is designed to help the reader understand how visuals can become *a vision of thinking.* Numerous case studies will be used to explain the complexities of the Language of Pictures.

CHAPTER 1

Visuals Are Meaningful

I see what my eyes see

My brain knows what I see . . .

But, not all visuals are the same!

Most adults assume that when they look at something such as a picture, a photograph, a real object, or an activity, they see the same thing that any other observer sees. For example, if an adult looks at a 5 x 8 white card and sees a bright red ball painted in the center of the card, she assumes that when a child looks at the card, the child sees and perceives the same object. Thus, if the adult shows the card to a child and the child looks at the card and doesn't name the object on the card, the adult assumes that the child sees the object on the card but does not have the label, "ball," to name it.

In reality, however, people learn the meaning of what they are able to ***perceive*** that they see or hear. Therefore, a child may look at the same card as the adult, but the child may only see the outline of a shape rather than the object (ball), or the child may see nothing at all on the card. The child's ability to see objects and people in real life or as pictures on cards occurs because the child learns the ***meaning*** of what he sees. Therefore, for a child to see an object like a ball on a card, the child has to do some learning. Meaning develops from personal learning.

Learning includes the process of acquiring the meaning of visuals, such as being able to see a ball on a card. This book, ***The Language of Pictures***, is a story designed to describe the process of acquiring visual meaning. Chapter 1 introduces the reader to the first part of the story. The first lesson of the story about the Language of Pictures is that "not all visuals are equal in meaning."

Visuals Are Not Equal in Meaning

No one wanted to work with Arnie, an 11-year-old male. He had no oral language. He didn't read. He didn't write. He could not imitate sounds, and he could not share conventional ways of communicating. He repeatedly scored around 35 on IQ tests, a score that is the lowest number given on some IQ tests. What could Arnie possibly do? What could support specialists do to help him? What could educators do to teach him?

Arnie was taught some American Sign Language as a preschooler but never used signing for language. Professionals worked with him on producing sounds, but at 11 years of age, his grunts and vocalizations did not approximate intelligible words. He knew no letters and no numbers. He did not know any pre-academic skills such as colors or shapes. After many years of educational intervention, most people assumed that Arnie was not able to do what educators expected. Therefore, most did not want to work with him.

Most recently, Arnie was assigned to a young practicum student who needed to gain some teaching experience. Instead of focusing on what he could not do, the practicum student looked for something Arnie *could do*; something they could communicate about. He could walk. He sat when others sat. He could use his back pocket comb to slick his hair down into a 1960s ducktail. He dressed himself and he tucked in his own crisp white shirttail and tied his own shoes. Arnie intently watched the practicum student's face when she spoke to him. He had been diagnosed with atresia, a closure of both ears and possible deformities of the middle or inner ear. He acted as if he could not hear speech, because he couldn't. Physically he was developing like an 11-year-old, and socially he attended to every detail the practicum student showed him. Even though his IQ score indicated that Arnie had not learned the language concepts (cognition) of an 11-year-old, his daily living skills, such as personal grooming, showed that he was able to learn.

This gap between Arnie's appropriate level of personal grooming and his reportedly low level of cognitive development left the practicum student perplexed. After all, developmental research suggests that a learner who demonstrates a certain level of development in one area should show the same level of development in other areas. For example, if Arnie could groom himself like an 11-year-old, he should speak like an 11-year-old.

Arnie's developmental profile did not fit what the literature suggested about development. He did not have developmental skills at the same level. On one hand, Arnie did not show the language or cognition of even a preschooler; on the other, he had the physical development of an 11-year-old and he could groom himself like an 11-year-old. Arnie learned grooming and some social skills, but he had not learned the expected academic abilities. Many knowledgeable and highly experienced professionals had provided him education through 11 years of state-of-the-art interventions. During this time, his diagnoses had ranged from severely emotionally disturbed with moderate hearing loss to autism to mental retardation. What could this volunteering practicum student offer Arnie?

Arnie, like most learners, knew what he could do. During the first session, he grabbed the practicum student's paper and more than once looked at what she was writing. How could she use this knowledge of what he *could do* to design an educational intervention based on his strengths? Remember, he didn't read, write, know letters, or produce intelligible speech. And he could not imitate any of these products or point to the pictures of any spoken or written concepts when asked to respond. His "point to the picture of X, Y or Z …" responses on a *Peabody Picture Vocabulary Test, Fourth Edition* (Dunn & Dunn, 2007) resulted in the same low-level score as his IQ test score. But Arnie's grabbing of the paper during the session and his attention to the practicum student's face and her writing, combined with his non-verbal grooming skills, demonstrated that Arnie was learning from "looking."

For the second session with Arnie, the practicum student brought them both pencils and plain paper to begin the communication process about something they could both see; after all, he seemed to attend to the paper and to what she wrote. But the young man beat her to the process that they would use. He brought her a drawing of a stock car. The drawing showed a street car with mirrors removed, numbers on the sides, doors welded, and so on. The practicum student, raised in a family of stock car race supporters, immediately knew that Arnie drew accurate information that was from his conceptual perspective, not a replication or imitation of someone else's drawing.

Arnie showed the practicum student the drawing of his car by pointing to various parts of the car, while producing unintelligible vocalizations. When he finished with his "show and tell," he neatly folded the picture and handed it to her. When she tried to unfold the drawing to use it for further communication, he pushed the folded paper back into her hand. So she said "thank you" and put his folded drawing away. She then pulled out a plain piece of paper, and they began to draw a different car. As she drew the car and manually signed concepts about the picture *within* his hand, his vocalizations began to become intelligible.

The young man that no one wanted to work with was able to use the drawings and their labels along with the motor hand signs to create clear motor patterns of speech. The literature had told the practicum student that learners first had to speak to be able to read, and then to write. In other words, a person's oral language comes from the production of sound. This same oral production is the basis for reading and writing. But Arnie's learning system followed a different process than the one suggested in the developmental literature.

He could not produce or follow the patterns of sound. He could follow the motor patterns of the practicum student's hand writing labels of the ideas on Arnie's drawing. He did the best productions of speech when the practicum student held his hand in her hand while they wrote labels onto the drawing, or when she signed (fingerspelled) the motor patterns of the labels of ideas as motor shapes into his hand for the concepts of the drawing. Arnie could feel the shape of the motor patterns of the hand that represented his drawn ideas of the car. Arnie's drawings showed that he could learn concepts.

How did Arnie learn these concepts or ideas that he could draw? He had not learned the visual-motor movements of sign language to talk about pictures. He had not learned to produce intelligible speech even though he had had considerable speech therapy for sound production, a visual-motor task of imitating sounds. He lacked conceptual understanding of others' pictures because he could not respond to commands such as "point to the number on the car door" or "point to the picture of a ball." Arnie could not use the sound of others' voices, and he could not connect visuals such as the object (ball) with the picture of a ball to the visual lips or hand movements of someone else. Arnie could not and did not use a picture communication assistive board that had been created for him. Arnie could not learn with sounds representing ideas or concepts and he could not learn with visuals representing concepts.

But when this practicum student took Arnie's hand into her hand and moved his hand through the hand-in-hand signs of what he drew, and could point to, then Arnie moved his mouth to match the movements of her mouth. Arnie's hand movements, coupled with Arnie's mouth movements, resulted in Arnie being able to produce intelligible word patterns. ***Arnie was acquiring concepts through motor acts***. Pictures alone, especially those produced by others, had little, if any, meaning to Arnie. Signs for concepts or letters or any other visuals did not produce mental pictures for Arnie. But Arnie could learn the concepts of The Language of Pictures if he could move his hands and mouth into the shape of ideas (more about this type of learning may be found later in this book and also in Arwood & Kaulitz, 2007).

It has been 40 years since that practicum student worked with Arnie. That practicum student is one of the authors, Ellyn Lucas Arwood. She has no idea what happened to Arnie, but she thinks about him often. It was Arnie who taught her many lessons about visuals: (a) Not everyone learns to speak, read, and write in that order; (b) Learners can acquire conceptual meanings or ideas before they can learn language – Arnie could learn concepts such as how to comb his hair even though he could not tell you about these concepts; (c) Natural (not replicated or imitated) samples of drawings represent a learner's underlying conceptual meaning; (d) The meaning of a drawing such as a stock car used for racing is unique to a person's learning, so drawing is not a conventional form of language; (e) Intelligence scores represent how well a person can learn language to represent concepts. If those teaching concepts don't teach in the same way a student learns concepts, then conceptual learning does not occur, and IQ scores will reflect that; and (f) Because each person is a story, focusing on the person's strengths provides a successful path to intervention.

But probably the biggest lesson that Arnie taught this author was that "***not all visuals are the same.***" For example, watching a person's hands move was not the same as seeing a stock car move at the track. Or watching a person's face make sounds was not the same as learning to write the words that went with the drawings. Or, imitating another person's mouth movements was not the same as talking about an idea.

Visuals offer varying kinds of information to different learners. In other words, the visual meaning of a picture requires an interpretation by the person who created the picture as well as by the person looking at the picture. And these interpretations are unique. For example, Arnie did not learn the names (signs or speech) for objects or for pictures of objects. When given a set of pictures and told to point to the comb, he could not point to the picture of a comb even though he could use a comb. The remainder of this chapter will discuss why not all visuals are the same.

> *Activity: Why was Arnie able to draw a picture but not able to point to pictures that others presented to him?*

Where Does the Meaning of a Visual Come From?

When a person looks at a picture, a graphic organizer, a photograph, or the objects of an activity, he sees only what he recognizes or is able to **perceive**. For example, an 11-year-old sixth grader, Forester, was looking at some pictures in a book and talking about what he saw in the pictures. Forester turned to an illustrated drawing of a boy sitting cross-legged on a stool in a kitchen-like setting. Staring at the picture, he asked, "Why is there a turkey?" The adult said, "Point to the turkey." Forester pointed to the boy's legs.

Understanding that perception is everything, the adult did a quick mental dance to try to understand what Forester was seeing. She then said, "Oh, yes, the crossed legs do have the shape of a turkey that you cook and eat at Thanksgiving; however, this is a face (pointed to the face of the boy) and this is the same boy that we saw on the other pages. In this picture, the boy has his legs crossed. See, here are his shoes. He is sitting on a stool. Do you know what a stool is?" Forester responded with a head shake. The adult then drew the three-legged stool on another piece of paper. Forester asked, "What is it?" She explained how the stool had three legs like the seat of a chair, and so on, and that it was for sitting. Forester could then talk about the stool but still could not see the boy in the picture. Figure 1.1 is an illustration of what the picture was like.

Figure 1.1. **A boy is sitting on a three-legged stool.**

Forester could not see the three-dimensional object represented by the picture because of the background and the stool being drawn in perspective. In other words, even though he was a general education sixth grader, he could not see a concept that did not match his meaning of what he knew about boys sitting in a kitchen. **To perceive the concepts of a picture, a person has to learn the meaning of a picture.**

Activity: Why did the boy have trouble seeing what was in the picture?

So, if perception is everything and seeing a visual requires the learning of meaning, where does perception come from? How does a person learn to perceive? Where does the learning of perception come from? Arnie taught the author that perception does not just develop but has to be learned. He could perceive the elements of shapes from motor movements but not the elements of sound or sight. So, how does perception occur through learning?

Four Levels of Learning Meaning

Perception is one of four levels of learning meaning acquired through the Neurosemantic Language Learning System (Arwood, 1991; Arwood & Kaulitz, 2007). The four levels of meaning are as follows:

1. *sensory* or cellular levels of *reception* of incoming sights, sounds, tastes, touches, smells (sensory receptors)

2. separation of the sensory input into *recognizable patterns* of meaning or *perceptions*

3. overlap of perceptual meanings into *concepts* or *conceptual meaning*

4. representation of the meaning of the concepts with the patterns of *language*

Forester could see something on the page (level one, sensory reception). His eyes were okay. He could hear the adult tell him what he was looking at because his hearing was okay. Furthermore, his sensory system for seeing and hearing had been tested, and his sensory reception was found to be okay. He could recognize the patterns (level two, or recognizable patterns) of what he saw as the shape of a turkey dressed for dinner, because he had concepts about turkey, but he did not have concepts (level three for conceptual meaning) about boys sitting on stools in a kitchen. So he was able to see what he had meaning for … not what someone else who drew the picture had meaning for. Also, Forester could use language to talk about what he could perceive from the picture, his language represented his perception of meaning, not the illustrator's meaning. He perceived and therefore saw a turkey, not a boy with his legs crossed sitting on a stool.

> *Activity: What are the four levels of the acquisition of meaning, according to Arwood's Neurosemantic Theory of Language Learning?*

Arnie and Forester and the Four Levels of Meaning

Forester could see and he could hear. He could talk and use language. But when looking at the picture of the boy sitting on a stool, Forester could only *perceive* the meaning of a turkey, something he knew; not the stool, something he did not know. So Forester needed more conceptual meaning about the picture before he could arrive at the intended meaning. By giving Forester more meaning about what he perceived, he could begin to understand what he was seeing in the picture.

On the other hand, Arnie could see what he perceived, but sound had little meaning for him. So intervention based on sound was not effective for him. Sound-based intervention, including saying the meaning of manual signs, reading the sounds of print on a page, pointing to pictures of named ideas, practicing the making of oral sounds for speech, and so on, was not effective. Arnie's development was restricted to being able to *perceive only what he had acquired through the learning of motor patterns,* not sounds or sounds to visuals.

He could draw a stock car because he saw the *movement* of a stock car over and over at the race track. The repetition of the movement of the car created the shape of the car for Arnie to be able to perceive. Arnie could draw a stock car, and the practicum student used Arnie's ability to draw what he perceived to help Arnie learn to see the shapes of other concepts or ideas. In other words, once Arnie could draw and recognize his drawing, then the practicum student could sign the concept (language) so that Arnie could learn the language for the concept. Then Arnie could produce (motor patterns) the name of the object by matching his own mouth movements (motor patterns) to the practicum student's mouth movements (motor patterns) to the hand-in-hand signing of the letter movements to form shapes. The overlap of the motor movements allowed Arnie to begin to conceptualize meaning for talking, reading, writing, and so on.

As soon as Arnie acquired the conceptual meanings of the names of what he drew through this motor process of learning, he could *perceive* the meaning of an object in other pictures. In short, Arnie learned the concepts through his own production of motor patterns of the shape of the hands, lips, and so on, to form concepts. Because few people had taught Arnie the concepts in the way his learning system created meaning of concepts, he had developed few concepts. Because Arnie acquired few concepts, he *could not see* the objects that others drew on a card, nor could he see the words on a page or someone else's hands moving through space, and so on. But Arnie learned the language of concepts he perceived from motor patterns that he formed into the shapes of concepts.

Arnie had a problem with the sensory input or the first level of neurosemantic meaning. Remember, he had atresia, which blocked receiving sound through air waves. This affected all the other levels of meaning. Furthermore, he could not learn concepts unless the recognizable patterns produced the shape of an idea such as hand-in-hand signing of a concept matched with the motor movements of the mouth. Arnie's Language of Pictures was dependent on learning how to create shapes or pictures of the motor movements.

Activity: Why did Arnie need to know the concept of a visual before he could recognize the visual?

Note: All people need to be able to recognize the conceptual meaning in a picture before they can share the same meaning for what they see.

Pictures for Arnie and Forester had different levels of meaning and would be interpreted according to what they knew. In other words, all materials represent a level of meaning. All visuals have a level of meaning. Arnie and Forester could interpret what pictures meant to them based on their levels of meaning. Arnie had few conceptual meanings. Forester possessed a lot of concepts but needed some refinement of his conceptual meaning.

Activity: Why do visual materials mean different ideas to different people?

All Visuals Have a Level of Meaning

All visual materials, activities, words, and pictures have meaning. Whether or not a learner can use the meaning depends on two factors: (a) how the person learns meaning; and (b) the level of meaning the visual has for the learner. Arnie learned only when the meaning came to him through his own motor movements. Forester learned by adding visual meanings to what he could see. The two boys had different ways to process meaning for learning, and they were functioning at two different levels. Therefore, *using different levels of visual materials and in different ways was important for these boys to learn.* Using the same type of pictures and visual interventions would not be successful.

Knowing that there are four basic acquisition levels of meaning is part of the story of learning visual meaning. An educator must also know the learner's level of meaning so as to be able to provide a picture or visual at the developmentally appropriate level. For example, Forester could recognize and use age-appropriate language for most grade-level materials, but he could not *see* ideas for which he did not have meaning. Arnie could not use others' pictures of objects because a visual representation of objects on a piece of paper did not create meaning for him. So, what does Arnie or Forester see, if they do not see what others see on a page? Arnie and Forester see what each has meaning for!

At the initial time of working with Arnie, he was able to only see the objects that he drew. In order to begin to see others' drawings, pictures, photographs, and so on, he had to learn to perceive the meaning of the visuals on the paper. He knew what he drew, but he did not see what others drew because he did not have the conceptualization of others' ideas. His conceptual learning was limited to what he could act on by drawing or performing. His motor movements created a perception of shape that allowed him to perceive the meaning of shapes.

Forester did not see what others would see in the picture of a boy sitting on a stool, because he did not have the same meaning for the boy's legs crossed on a stool. However, he did have the meaning for crossed turkey legs that he eats at Thanksgiving.

Both boys needed more learning to be able to perceive specific types of visuals. And each boy learned concepts in a different way of connecting patterns. Arnie connected motor patterns to form visual shapes of ideas. Forester connected visual patterns to form visual shapes of ideas.

Learning to Sense: Stage One

All babies are born unable to see ideas on a piece of paper or to hear the spoken words of another person. But if the baby has normal sensory receptors, eyes, ears, nose, skin, and mouth, the baby uses sensory input to learn the meaning of sounds, sights, tastes, touches, and smells. The baby's sensory organs physically connect the child to his or her environment. The environment provides a continuous stream of acoustic features, visual features, taste options, pressures of touch, and olfactory arrays of input. Two of these sensory inputs are closely linked to human language, the acoustic and the visual. Acoustic input comes in the form of the sound wave. The sound wave consists of the following components: the speed of the wave or frequency of pitch, such as how high or low a voice appears; the height of the wave or the amplitude of loudness; and the time between waves or duration. Figure 1.2 shows the components of a sound wave.

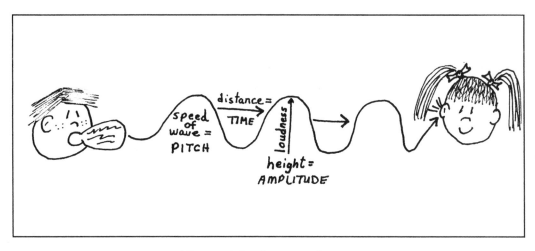

Figure 1.2. **The sound wave.**

The baby's ear and the pathways that take sound from the ear to the brain are designed to recognize these three acoustic features: pitch, loudness, and duration. So, when a baby hears the sounds of a person's voice, the baby is hearing the separate sound features of the voice. Voices are not words. Voices are noises much like the sound of an unknown machine running in the background. Therefore, background sounds such as the fan of a heater may have equal acoustic meaning to the newborn as a parent's voice. The baby is learning to process the meaning of the different features of sound.

Meaningful sensory features, like those that make up sound, continue to come into the learning system through the sensory receptor organs, ear, eye, nose, mouth, and skin. Over time the features overlap to create patterns that become recognizable clusters (for an explanation of visual pathways, see Logothetis, 2007). For example, most babies can recognize familiar voice features of caregivers within the first couple of months, but even though the baby recognizes the voice, the meaning of the spoken words of the voice is not learned until later.

The visual wave is a light wave. The light wave has features or characteristics just like the sound wave. Light waves are generated from a source of energy like the sun or a light. The features of the light wave consist of particles of energy that reflect off the edge of planes (see Figure 1.3).

Figure 1.3. The light wave.

As more particles reflect, more spots on the surface of the object or plane are lit up. Eventually, the entire surface of an object lights up as a pattern. These patterns overlap and form the shapes of objects. As a baby moves physically through space or moves his or her eyes, the baby is able to see more and more sets of visual patterns, and is able to see the physical properties of familiar objects by around 4 to 6 months. (For an explanation of the movements of eyes, see Martinez-Conde & Macknik, 2007.) By 3 years of age, most children can look at themselves in a three-way mirror and begin to wonder who that person is whose backside is displayed in the mirror. The child is learning that he or she has a front and a back. Again, a child will only know what the child recognizes as patterns of input. When the child asks who is in the mirror, the adult quickly responds with, "Oh, that is you … see … here is your front and here is your back." Usually, the child will turn her head over her shoulder to try to catch a glimpse of her backside in the mirror.

For a child to be able to recognize the meaning of a visual, the child has to have more than sensory input. The child also has to be able to perceive the recognized patterns formed from the sensory input and then be able to attach conceptual meaning to the visual patterns. Much of the conceptual meaning is assigned from caregivers, similar to the example of the mirror. Whether or not a child can *perceive* or recognize the assigned meaning depends on how the adult inputs the meaning.

Activity: Sensory inputs form perceptions. When is a child able to perceive the sensory input?

Learning to Perceive: Stage Two

Sensory input comes from the eyes, ears, nose, mouth, and/or skin. From these sensory inputs come the perceptual patterns to create concepts. This process of cells bringing sensory input into the perceptual processing for cognitive brain development is meaningful to each learner according to how the child's neurology functions. Arwood calls this learning process the Neurosemantic Language Learning Theory (Arwood, 1983, 1991). Neurosemantic language learning refers to the physical process of learning the language of meaning through recognition of perceptual patterns from sensory input to form concepts.

For example, a mother regularly combs her 5-month-old baby's hair. One morning, the baby is propped up on a pillow seat. While the mother reaches for some clothes, the baby reaches the comb and puts the comb to her hair. The fact that the comb is upside down and that the young child lacks the coordination to actually comb her hair is not as important as the fact that the baby has the learning system to do what she has seen her mother do over and over and over. Most babies who can learn concepts by watching someone else are able to connect visual patterns together to form concepts. Some research suggests that individuals with autism spectrum disorders (ASD) may lack some of the cells or structures (e.g., mirror neurons; see Ramachandran & Oberman, 2006; Rizzolatti, Fogassi, & Gallese, 2006) to be able to imitate what others do. This means that a child with ASD who lacks this ability to learn visual concepts through visual imitation will need input about visual scenarios such as social learning presented in different ways than through visual imitation. Likewise, most children with ASD are able to visually construct mental meaning, but often are like Arnie; they need to create that visual meaning through the overlap of motor patterns, not the imitation of sound or sight.

> ### *Activity: Are most children with ASD able to use imitation of what they see or hear to develop concepts?*

In addition to seeing what the mother, in the above example, does with the comb, the baby receives other sensory input. For example, the mother talks to her baby while she is grooming her. So, the baby is receiving sensory input not only through the eyes from what she sees but also through the eyes from what Mother says. When the baby is about 9 months old, the baby says "ka" as she reaches for the comb. The baby is able to take the sound of the mother's assigned meaning and pair it with the visual object. This baby is able to combine visual and acoustic sensory input to begin to develop an auditory concept that is named with language, "comb." This ability to connect sound and sight means that this baby can learn concepts through the input of acoustic and visual patterns to produce speech that matches what others say around the baby.

Individuals on the spectrum do not use this type of input for concepts. Some are not able to imitate what they hear for speech. Others pick up the acoustic properties of sound for speech and imitate speech very well but fail to connect the sound with the visual objects so they cannot learn concepts from the imitation of sound. Some children on the autism spectrum learn lots of acoustic patterns but need a great deal of intervention to make the acoustic patterns into naturally spoken words or concepts. Children who learn the acoustic patterns without visual meaning echo what they hear without underlying conceptualization or meaning. ***Acoustic patterns by themselves do not lead to language.***

If a child cannot connect what she sees with what she hears, she may not be able to develop expected academic or social skills. For example, she might not be able to understand the sounds of decoding print or the social meanings of visuals such as people's faces. Individuals diagnosed on the autism spectrum do not simultaneously connect sound with sight to form auditory concepts. Therefore, they also show difficulty with some of the expected academic and/or social skills.

So, some children and adults can use visual patterns to form concepts, and some can use acoustic and visual patterns, but most individuals diagnosed with ASD learn concepts the way Arnie did. Like Arnie, the shape of an idea is more important to them than the sight of what they see. These shapes develop through the reflection of light on the edge of a plane or from the movement of eyes or body across the visual plane (like an edge) of an object. In other words, the edge of a bubble of a word is easier for them to see than the letters inside the bubble. Figure 1.4 shows how edges of an idea create a shape.

Figure 1.4. **The bubble shape of an idea.**

Arnie was only able to perceive the meaning of a picture when he made the picture himself. To be able to make a picture, his learning system required numerous motor experiences from which he built visual concepts. Eventually, Arnie saw the edges of the car, and then he was able to draw the shapes of what he saw as the car. His visual perception came from seeing the edges of light reflecting off the movement of objects, such as the car moving around the track over and over and over. So the shapes of ideas for Arnie came from the movements of what he could see.

Unlike Arnie, Forester could talk. He was able to learn some acoustic patterns for what he heard others say. He was also able to see the ideas of what he physically experienced. He had learned a lot of what he had seen and heard, but he was not able to see the content of a picture for which he did not have the meaning at a conceptual level.

Forester needed the development of concepts for the picture he was looking at and Arnie needed to acquire the patterns of concepts that he moved through. Arnie and Forester remind us that all visuals have meaning, but the level of meaning depends on the level of conceptualization for what a person is looking at.

People can only see what they perceive from the incoming patterns of sensory input. Perception comes from the sensory patterns to form what a person knows conceptually. So if a child like Arnie does not see a shape on a card, the child does not perceive the shape. This is not a labeling problem. This is a conceptual limitation as a result of failure to perceive the input in the way the learner creates meaning. *Language represents the concepts. Language for the concept will come from learning to perceive the meaning.*

> *Activity: What are some perceptual (patterns of input) options for seeing something?*

Learning Concepts: Stage Three

As we have seen, the first level of acquisition of meaning is sensory input. In stage two, the various inputs overlap to form patterns of recognition. When these patterns sufficiently overlap, the child begins to show concept development or understanding, arriving at stage three. For example, a baby reaches for Mother's comb and then looks up at Mother and looks back at the comb. The child is nonverbally showing a level of understanding of what she sees. She sees the relationships among the comb (object), Mother (agent), and the comb's activity (action). Nonverbally, the child shows an understanding of basic semantic relationships – meaningful relationships among agents, actions, and objects. In this way, the child is beginning to show her understanding of concepts. This ability to learn concepts continues over time. Each time a child acquires more meaning of a concept, the child also acquires greater understanding of a concept. Figure 1.5 shows the stages of conceptual meaning.

Ages 0-2	Ages 2-7	Ages 7-11	Ages 11 and older
Sensori-Motor Level Represents underlying semantic relations or single ideas such as: 	**Preoperational Level** Represents the child as an agent in his/her picture of multiple actions and objects in an event such as: 	**Concrete Level** Represents multiple agents and multiple actions for multiple events such as: 	**Formal Level** Represents ideas that have multiple mental visuals or words such as "respect." 
Jane plays with the ball.	Jane throws the ball to Mom.	Jane works with her classmates.	Respect

Figure 1.5. **Stages of conceptual meaning.**

Activity: What are the four stages of conceptual development? Reminder: These are stages within the four stages or levels of neurosemantic language learning.

Learning Language: Stage Four

The fourth stage of acquisition of meaning is learning language. As the child acquires concepts and begins to act on the concepts, caregivers provide language for what the child perceives and begins to know. For example, the child looks at the comb and back at the mother's face, and the mother says, "Yes, that is your comb. Let's comb your pretty hair." These acoustic patterns are new sensory inputs for the child's brain to recognize and connect to past patterns. As these present and past visual and acoustic patterns overlap, the child begins to put a language pattern, such as "comb," to the underlying perception of the object and its function. As early as 9 months, the child looks at the comb and says, "Ko me ai," which is "Comb my hair." The child is beginning to show the acquisition of language meaning to represent the underlying concepts formed from recognized perceptual patterns.

Activity: Where does language come from?

Application of the Stages of Visual Meaning to Learning

Because all materials, visuals, instructions, curricula, and so on, have a level of meaning, a visual may have meaning at one of the four described levels of neurosemantic meaning (Arwood, 1991). One child could look at a picture and see no concepts, only sensory input such as a blank piece of paper. Another child looks at the same picture and sees the sensory input as a set of patterns that form an unknown shape. A third child looks at the same picture and sees the shape of an object that looks like a hamburger and says "It's a hamburger." Finally, a fourth child looks at the same picture and asks, "What kind of flying saucer is this?"

For child one, the child's level of meaning for the picture is at a sensory level. The second child is able to recognize patterns from past sensory input, but she does not perceive or recognize the patterns. She is at a perceptual level of meaning. The third child sees an object and knows the meaning of the shape as a "hamburger," something the child eats. This child is at a conceptual level of meaning, but the child is not at the same conceptual level of meaning as the fourth child. The fourth child is able to see what an adult sees when he looks at the picture. This child sees a spaceship, not a hamburger. This fourth child asks a question about the spaceship, which means he is able to use language to learn more about concepts.

Activity: What are the four stages of conceptual meaning as they relate to language development?

Learning and Language for Pictures or Visuals

Because each child learns the meaning of what he or she sees based on what he or she knows, each child knows only what he or she perceives within a picture. In other words, visuals have different levels of meaning based on what the person who uses the visual is able to understand about what he or she sees in the visual. Furthermore, because visuals are different in meaning for different learners, they must be used differently for different students. How well a student is able to see what is in the picture determines how well he is able to learn from the picture or visual.

As children learn more about concepts, they are able to learn more from the pictures. That is, the pictures do not need to include as much information if the learner brings more information to the picture. However, just because a child can see there is a picture on a piece of paper does not mean the child is learning the concept about what he sees. Being able to see is the first level of sensory input. Recognizing that there is a visual is a second level or perceptual level. So, perception is based on being able to see the visual. However, when a child perceives the meaning of the visual, the child is physically able to begin to create a concept about the visual. Concepts occur in layers of meaning. Therefore, meaning can be added to concepts across four levels or stages. Language patterns represent the meaning of the concepts.

Activity: How does learning and language relate to the stages of meaning and to conceptualization?

Most children with ASD have difficulty turning everyday patterns of perception into concepts, since most patterns are *not* presented the way these children learn. To learn language, a child with ASD must be able to create visual concepts – either from the motor movements that create shapes of ideas or from the visual patterns that form concepts. In this way, a child learns language the way she is able to create concepts.

Summary

This knowledge about various levels of meaning helps us write a story about the Language of Pictures. Pictures are visuals that have different levels of meaning. And since learners like Arnie and Forester possess different ways to process the input, they acquire different meanings based on their different learning systems. Understanding the level of meaning for materials as well as the different levels of meaning and learning of the children helps parents and educators adjust their interventions to match what the children's learning levels are. Furthermore, not only making visuals match the level of meaning the child possesses but also providing the visuals in the way a child learns meaning helps increase the success of intervention. Chapter 2 will provide more understanding of how visuals provide language meaning.

Activity: Do visuals mean something different to different people? If so, why? If not, why not? How does language represent concepts?

CHAPTER 2
Language Provides Meaning for Visuals

Thinking in pictures!

So you think you know what I see …

But do you have my language for my pictures?

My pictures are unique; your language is conventional.

When looking at a picture, most people assume that everyone else sees what they see. But the reality is that each person's perception of what he or she sees is unique. Chapter 1 began the story of the Language of Pictures by introducing the notion that a person sees only learned meanings. Since we all experience different events in life, we all experience unique meanings and, therefore, different perceptions of the same picture. Language assigns the interpreted meaning of one's perceptions. This chapter will discuss the way people assign meaning to pictures through language.

Where Does the Language of a Picture Come From?

Thirty teachers are sitting around tables in an open media center listening to a workshop on language. The presenter explains how students create mental visuals in response to the oral language of the teacher. The teachers understand that their students think in visuals, but they do not understand that when the teacher draws a picture of a concept, the students are able to obtain more meaning about what the teacher is saying.

The presenter wants the teachers to begin to understand how their drawing in the classroom is meaningful to the student, so the presenter asks the teachers to draw their own ideas of "Columbus." The teachers begin to draw. Some of them look at other teachers' pictures to see what they are drawing. The presenter reminds them that this is an independent task and that each teacher is to draw his or her own idea of "Columbus."

The presenter looks around and sees that no two pictures are alike, which is what she expected since no two teachers have the same learning experiences about "Columbus." Some teachers' drawings are of ships or boats, other drawings are of land masses; some drawings are of people, others are of maps, and so forth. After a few minutes, the presenter tells the teachers to orally share their pictures with each other. Interestingly, as the teachers share their drawings, they begin to argue with one another about the pictures, whether what they drew was "right" or "wrong." Each teacher believes that his or her perception is "right." And, of course, each teacher's perception is unique, which makes his or her drawing unique. Each teacher's drawing represents his or her perception of his or her personal learning about "Columbus." And, all perceptions are valid!

The bottom line is that pictures can't be "right" or "wrong." What each teacher drew is an interpretation of each teacher's personal perception of Columbus. And, what each teacher sees in other teachers' drawings is also an interpretation of what each person perceives or knows about the other teacher's drawing. To talk about the pictures or to explain the drawings is based on language. Each teacher put language to his or her understanding of the concept, Columbus. That is, each teacher interpreted what he or she thought about the concept. The drawings represented the meaning each teacher mentally thought about when given the word, Columbus. Each teacher interpreted the meaning of the concept of Columbus through language. For one teacher the concept of Columbus referred to a man, so she drew a picture of a man. For someone else, the concept of Columbus referred to an historic voyage, so that teacher drew ships. Thirty different meanings were assigned to "Columbus" because there were 30 different teachers.

This chapter will focus on how all visuals represent the unique properties of a concept and how language interprets these conceptual meanings. *All visuals provide an opportunity to use language to increase the meaning of a concept or to better understand a concept.*

Activity: How do drawings represent a person's perception? Is it possible to have a variety of perceptions for the same concept? Why?

Language Emerges from Learning Concepts

Language represents what a person thinks or knows. Thinking or knowing occurs in the form of concepts. So, when a person sees a picture, the person interprets what he or she sees based on what he or she thinks or knows. That is, from what the person thinks or conceptualizes. Figure 2.1 shows a child looking at a picture and thinking about what he sees. Note that the adult who is sitting across from the child also is thinking about the picture, but they do not have the same thought about what they see. The child and the adult think in different meanings about the same picture.

Figure 2.1. **Different people look at the same picture but have different thoughts about it.**

Activity: Why does a picture represent a person's thoughts?

These different thoughts or ideas are called concepts. A learner thinks in a system of concepts. When a learner sees a visual like a drawing or picture, the learner's sensory organs take in the input that will eventually form concepts. So each learner creates a concept that represents the unique properties that he or she recognizes as meaningful. Since all sensory input is different, all patterns that form concepts are unique. Concept development, therefore, is unique to a learner.

Language is the tool that connects one person's unique concepts with another person's unique concepts. Figure 2.2. shows how the child and adult have different concepts or different mental ideas about trees. But this time the adult shares her language with the child, "This is a beautiful tree." The child adds his language, "It's by my house." In this way, language connects the two different mental ideas to the same picture. Their different perceptions about the picture result in two different concepts, which are then bridged through language.

Figure 2.2. **Language connects different mental ideas.**

If the teachers who were arguing about the rightness or wrongness of their drawings had understood that their pictures show the unique development of each person's concept of "Columbus," they could have used language to determine what each person knew or didn't know about Columbus. For example, one teacher could see the other person's drawing and connect her picture of a person to the picture of an island, "Oh, that's true. Columbus did land on some islands." All of the teachers' different ideas could be overlapped to arrive at a greater understanding of the concept "Columbus." In other words, with shared language, the teachers could all learn more about their conceptualization of Columbus. *Language bridges and refines the meaning of concepts.*

┌───┐
│ *Activity: Give an example of how language can connect multiple ideas about a topic.* │
└───┘

Language used with visuals, such as personal drawings, can provide greater conceptual meaning for all individuals, especially those who are diagnosed with an autism spectrum disorder (ASD) since their conceptualization is visual in nature. Individuals with ASD, just like the teachers in the media center, are often surprised to find out that they are visually making a mental picture that is different from that of another person. Figure 2.3 shows the response of a student who misunderstands what the teacher means because he does not realize that her pictures (what she knows) does not match what he knows.

Figure 2.3. **The child thinks the teacher has the same mental pictures he has.**

The student expects the adult to see what he mentally sees. He sees himself singing at his audition. The teacher doesn't know anything about his audition. When the teacher asks for clarification, the student interprets the question as an indication that the teacher won't come. Figure 2.4 shows the next interpretation of the mental mismatch of concepts between the teacher and student.

Figure 2.4. **The teacher uses language to try to bridge what she doesn't know with what he knows.**

Finally, in Figure 2.5, the written language bridges what the student thinks with what the teacher knows so that his ideas are connected to the teacher's ideas.

Figure 2.5. The teacher draws and writes the language to begin to connect the child's pictures with the teacher's pictures.

Activity: Do people ever have the same mental pictures for the same topic? Why or why not?

As we have seen, what a person mentally sees in a visual is based on his or her perceptions of the represented concepts. *Language represents concepts.* When one draws concepts, the drawings represent what a person uniquely thinks or knows about an idea, whereas the written words about the drawings represent a *conventional language* explanation of the concepts. Visuals that depict the concepts or ideas provide language for the person who thinks with visual concepts.

Language Represents Thinking

Language is a tool that represents a person's underlying thinking. So if a person thinks in pictures, his or her oral language is a translation of his mental concepts. The mental concepts are visual, but the oral (spoken) language is in sound. This mismatch between the thinking in visuals and a person's spoken language requires a translation for the person to be able to live, work, and go to school using English. Either the person is translating the sound of his voice into mental pictures or translating mental visuals into the sound of oral language. Since translations use interpreted meaning, there is also the possibility of a misperception of others' spoken ideas and/or a misconception of one's own ideas. Figure 2.6 shows how the translation process uses an interpretation of meaning.

Figure 2.6. The child hears Dad's voice but is not able to translate his words into matching visual concepts.

The child mentally thinks about school, but he is at home. This mismatch of concepts results in confusion, frustration, and even behavior management issues. Dad cannot figure how to move his son from the living room to the car to go to school. Notice that the child has a concept of what Dad says that is the child's perception of the sound of Dad's voice. Dad has a concept of what he means when he thinks about "going to school." Both Dad and his son have different concepts of the same oral, spoken language. Dad needs to change his spoken words to create mental pictures for his son, thereby using language to bridge the mismatch of perceptions to create shared concepts about going to school. Figure 2.7 shows how Dad's use of language changes the visual meaning for the son.

Figure 2.7. **Dad uses language to change the child's visual meanings.**

> *Activity: How did Dad help translate the auditory phrase "Let's go to school" into language that helped create visual mental pictures for the son?*

Notice that the more words the dad uses, the more meaning or visuals the son is able to create. With enough words or language, the son is able to make visual thoughts that match Dad's meaning. In this way, the dad's language provides clarity of meaning by helping create mental visuals. *Language provides meaning for the mental visuals as well as for the drawn visuals and connects the concepts of mental pictures between two or more speakers.* More language, not less, is important to help translate and connect unique mental perceptions into shared meanings. In this case, more language is added by drawing and writing, two visual-motor ways of adding meaning to the child's perception and therefore more shared conceptualization between the son and his dad.

> *Activity: Why is more, not less, language needed to make the mental pictures for the son?*

Language Provides Meaning for Pictures

Language consists of streams of written or spoken units that represent multiple underlying concepts. Just increasing the use of words, either spoken or written, does not necessarily clarify the underlying conceptual meaning. Figure 2.8 shows the use of "lots of words" as the child with ASD becomes overwhelmed by the barrage of sound. The sound of Mom's voice creates the mental picture of the blocks going away and nothing else. The child begins to flap and scream.

Figure 2.8. **Mom's words increase in number, but the meaning of her words does not create mental pictures.**

In the scenario shown in Figure 2.8, the language is not provided in a way the child understands. Mom's sounds do not make meaning. Whether or not language provides meaning to visuals depends on some basic language rules:

1. The person who draws or creates a picture draws from his or her own understanding of meaning, not someone else's meaning (e.g., Columbus).

2. The person looking at a picture or visual understands only what he or she has meaning for (see Figure 2.9).

Figure 2.9. **The child draws what the child knows.**

3. The mental image of a concept may not match spoken words (see Figure 2.10).

Figure 2.10. **This person's words do not match with what the other person drew. His underlying meaning is different.**

Visual Thinking Strategies

4. The words of a speaker may not match another person's mental pictures (see Figure 2.11).

Figure 2.11. The child hears, "Get on your coat!" So he gets <u>on</u> his coat.

5. Concepts determine actions and are unique. In Figure 2.12, the young man knows the patterns of what to say, "I am social," but his behavior shows that he does not know that when he passes a friend and doesn't look at and acknowledge him in some way, the friend does not think he is being friendly. In other words, the young man has social skills as rules but not as concepts.

Figure 2.12. "**I am social.**"

6. Language connects the pictures with the words only when both are used together so that perception of meaning matches the concepts. Figure 2.13 shows how language clarifies a child's conceptual meaning.

Figure 2.13. **Specific language can create mental pictures as a way to clarify meaning.**

Language Meaning

Because language represents concepts, language can be used to help clarify a child's mental visual concepts. For example, a teacher says, "Take out your books and turn to page 84." The teacher assumes that since they are talking about math, the students will take out their math books and turn to page 84 in the math book. But the word "book" is an oral pattern that retrieves a mental picture for John that is different from the teacher's mental picture. John thinks of his library book, *Harry Potter,* so he takes his Harry Potter book out of his desk and begins to read where he left off. Melanie, who is a diagnosed with autism, begins to say "page 84" over and over and over while she thumbs through her papers. Figure 2.14 shows how John and Melanie have different thoughts in response to the teacher's words.

Figure 2.14. **The teacher assumes that the children are "on the same page."**

John and Melanie possess mental concepts that do not match what the teacher expects them to do in response to her spoken language patterns. Both children need more language to connect their concepts to the teacher's oral patterns. They need to "see" what the teacher's words mean, and they need to "see" which language patterns go with which word meanings.

Figure 2.15 shows Melanie and John acquiring more meaning as the teacher uses richer language so that the patterns and concepts are closer to matching. Notice that Melanie and John still have slightly different mental images, but as the teacher uses more specific, visual-thinking types of words, both children are able to comply. Their understanding of what the teacher says matches what the teacher expects their behavior to look like. In this way, the patterns of spoken sound are connected to the mental pictures or concepts. And their compliance allows both Melanie and John to begin to connect what they mentally see to what the teacher says they have to do.

Figure 2.15. **The teacher changes her words to better create a mental picture for her students.**

Language provides patterns for concepts so that concepts can be refined in meaning. Language provides additional meaning so that a child gains better conceptualization, which in turn allows for better use of language. The art of assigning meaning to what a child knows and then waiting for the child's response to assign new meaning is like a "mental dance." That is, the child says something or does something and the adult assigns meaning to the child's acts using language. The child's meaning increases as the adult assigns more meaning. With more meaning, the child's language increases so that the child is able to use his own language to think with higher conceptualization. But remember that in order for the child to gain meaning from the adult, the adult's assigned meaning must be presented in the way that enables the child to create concepts. So if the teacher wants students to take out their math books, for example, she must use visual types of language to assign meaning to the task so that the students who think in visual concepts can make mental pictures that match the meaning of the teacher's words.

Activity: Why do words not always create a mental concept of what the speaker intended?

The Mental Dance of Language with Visuals

Different people think with different visual images for the same spoken concepts, and the spoken patterns of the speaker's or listener's oral language may or may not match the meaning of specific mental pictures. Connecting the conventional language to the mental visuals of a learner is a mental dance that moves back and forth between what the learner knows and doesn't know and what the teacher or parent knows and is able to represent with language. Helping create the Language of Pictures is a story that involves the steps of a dance.

Let's look at a dance about the Language of Pictures between a child and her tutor. First, the tutor says, "Rochele, it is good to see you. Let's go to the table to do our work." Now it is the child's turn to respond. The child says "bugga, bugga, bugga" and begins to look away while she stares at her flicking fingers. A third person who knows nothing about Rochele or the tutor and who is watching Rochele's "first dance step" might immediately think, "Rochele must not have any language." But the reality is that Rochele and her tutor are not dancing the same dance. For example, Rochele could be doing the steps to a waltz while her tutor is doing a tap dance. To do the same dance, they have to have a shared understanding of meaning. They have to share the choreography of the dance. The tutor's words that represent the tutor's thoughts need to relate and connect to Rochele's thoughts. To do the same dance, they must be in the same picture together doing the movements of the shared or agreed-upon dance. To do so, each person has to understand what his or her responsibilities in the dance are.

The tutor expects Rochele to come to the table with the same mental pictures the tutor has for what they will do together. But Rochele is thinking about the yucky sandwich she had for lunch. In order for the dance between the mental visuals that Rochele is thinking and the mental visuals about working at the table that the tutor is thinking, the adult must lead Rochele. To find a common or shared meaning, the adult draws out the previous "shared" event, lunch. Rochele watches the teacher draw and sees herself eating lunch. To this picture (Figure 2.16), Rochele says "bugga, bugga" and points to the lunch.

Figure 2.16. **Language assigns meaning to some visuals.**

Because Rochelle responds to the drawing by pointing and making an utterance, it is apparent that she sees herself in the drawing. The sound of Rochele's vocalizations indicates what she knows. So now that the teacher can see what Rochele knows and is "referring" to, the teacher can lead Rochele through what her mental visual concepts mean in language. To do so, the teacher draws out the meaning of the pictures while also attaching language to the pictures. In this way, the teacher connects the patterns of language to the pictured concepts related to Rochele's own experience.

This may not be enough meaning for Rochele, however. The teacher may need to draw hand-over-hand with Rochele as well as provide additional opportunities for her to learn the language through movement, such as writing. For example, the teacher may have to use more specific words, a lot more relational language, or to cartoon more, so that multiple pictures or conceptual meanings are assigned to the written patterns of language (Arwood & Kaulitz, 2007). In this way, overlapping language will create more concepts for Rochele. How well Rochele is able to respond to the meaning or the Language of Pictures provides an assessment of her developmental level of cognition, language, and socialization. Rochele is able to follow the dance steps of this event and is able to acquire the language for bridging what she knows with what the adult expects.

In the case of Rochele, the visual mental pictures of the teacher and Rochele are different, and each has different interpretations of the drawings. That is, Rochele wants to use the situation to continue to process her experience about the yucky lunch, whereas the teacher wants to teach something else during this time. Because of Rochele's level of understanding, the teacher takes the lead and uses what she can draw to begin to connect what Rochele knows with the teacher's written language. In this way, she begins to help Rochele see what the adult sees. The adult sees Rochele come to therapy, so that is the mental picture that the adult possesses. In order to "do therapy" with Rochele, the teacher must create a shared meaning between Rochele's perception of lunch and the teacher's expected concept of "therapy time." Because Rochele thinks using visual concepts, she needs pictures and writing to help learn the language.

Activity: Why do pictures need written or oral language added to them?

Perception and Conception

The teachers early in this chapter who drew what they knew about "Columbus" were representing their perceptions about a concept, Columbus. When they argued about their perceptions, they were trying to make the concept of Columbus have only one meaning. Since the concept of Columbus consists of multiple perceptions of who he was, what he did, when he did what he did, where he did what he did, and so forth, these teachers needed additional information to be able to accept multiple view points or perception about a concept.

Language could be used to help them begin to connect the multiple, different perceptions into a larger concept of Columbus. These teachers probably had many similar experiences about Columbus in their academic training, but because of their unique pasts, each created a different conceptual meaning for Columbus. Furthermore, when they looked at their colleagues' drawings, they could not understand why their colleagues did not draw what they had drawn. They did not understand that learning comes from assigning meaning to what one experiences.

These teachers have children in their classrooms who create their unique perceptions of the teachers' lesson, and therefore develop their own unique meanings for concepts. Because these teachers had lots of language, they could argue about the meaning of what they drew and begin to use their language to develop more conceptualization for "Columbus."

Rochele, on the other hand, had many unique perceptions but not enough language to create a shared conception of therapy with the teacher. She could not argue about the agenda of therapy. In fact, she did not have enough language to follow what the teacher expected for her to do in therapy. In order for Rochele to be able to follow the teacher's language, Rochele would have to have more meaning attached to her perceptions about lunch and how those perceptions connect to form a concept about therapy expectations. More language of the pictures about lunch connected to the pictures about the event of therapy will help Rochele begin to organize her perceptions into more of a concept of therapy so she can share in the therapy expectation of the teacher.

Summary

Language helps assign more conventional meaning to visuals. Language is a set of patterns that can be (a) spoken with specific visual types of words, (b) spoken with a lot of nonauditory words, and/or (c) written. Children with ASD need to have the language written for them and the concepts drawn so that they can begin to "see" the conventional meaning of their behavior, whether verbal or nonverbal. Without language assigning meaning to pictures, the pictures represent only what a person knows or doesn't know about a concept. *Language always interprets what a person sees in a picture or draws in a picture.* Therefore, drawings represent what a person knows, and looking at a picture and interpreting what is in the picture tells a parent or an educator what a child knows.

When interpreting pictures and when drawing pictures, the Language of the Pictures is important.

1. The person who draws or creates a picture draws from his or her own understanding of meaning, not someone else's meaning (e.g., Columbus).

2. The person looking at a picture or visual understands only what he or she has meaning for.

3. The mental image of a concept may not match the person's spoken words.

4. A spoken word or concept may have multiple visual perceptions or concepts related to the spoken word.

5. The meanings of concepts are unique because each person has unique past perceptions that create the concepts.

6. Language connects mental pictures with shared or conventional words that increase the meaning of one's mental concepts … through drawing, writing, and/or speaking, listening, viewing, calculating, and thinking.

Chapter 3 explains how a person's use of language demonstrates his or her level of conceptualization. By knowing a learner's level of conceptualization, a parent or educator can adjust the input of visuals and oral language to match the child's ability to think in concepts or to use visuals for thinking and for language.

CHAPTER 3

The Language Levels of Pictures

The child looks into the picture to see the bee,

but he sees a fly ...

Why does he not see the bee?

Because a bee flies?

On the path to discovering the Language of Pictures, Chapter 1 emphasized that a child perceives what the child conceptually knows when looking at a picture. "Knowing" evolves from our perceptions of experiences. Since we all have unique experiences, we also have unique perceptions. Therefore, different people see different ideas when they look at the same pictures. In other words, people who are looking at visuals have a certain level of meaning that they use to interpret what they see in pictures, based on their past experiences and what they know.

Chapter 1 also explained how a learner acquires knowledge of meaning through stages of neurobiological acquisition. Through these stages of acquiring meaning, a child learns to perceive patterns that eventually create concepts. Perceptions develop from experiences that overlap to create concepts or ideas, and language represents those concepts or ideas (Chapter 2). The more a child knows about a concept, the better she is able to develop language to refine her knowledge or to express what she knows.

Adults can use knowledge about the Language of Pictures to develop strategies to improve a child's thinking. But a child will only be able to use the Language of Pictures if he can perceive the meaning of the pictures. Therefore, to use pictures to help children learn concepts and develop language, educators and parents must consider the learner's level of language as well as the picture's level of language. This chapter provides information about the language levels of pictures.

Learning to See – Stage One of the Language Level of Pictures

Babies are born able to see but have no knowledge about what they see. Therefore, they do not see people, picture content, objects, and so forth. Babies learn to see people, objects, and pictures based on what their eyes record as experiences. Babies' eyes bring to their brains small bits of information in features of sight. The eyes, like the other receptor organs, bring bits of meaning to create a baby's perception of experience. These experiences, or patterns of perception, connect so that the baby "begins to see" an object or "begins to hear" a voice, after repeated, similar experiences.

After repeated experiences looking at Mom's facial features, the baby begins to recognize the meaning of those features. Likewise, the patterns of multiple sounds connect so the baby begins to recognize Mom's voice after multiple experiences of hearing the features of Mom's voice. ***The newborn baby learns to see only what meaning the environment provides and only what meaning the baby's neurobiological system of reception and processing is able to recognize, such as familiar objects or voices.***

Activity: The earliest development of knowledge comes from what types of features?

With constant sensory input, the baby learns to respond differently to the various inputs. For example, as the baby grows, she extends an arm and Mom puts a bottle in the child's hand to help her hold a bottle; subsequently, the baby begins to reach for a bottle because the baby is beginning to see Mom and beginning to see the bottle. The baby also begins to see her own hands, the movements of those hands, and even some of the features of Mom's face. Similarly, the baby begins to hear Mom's voice in the background. ***The baby's sensory experiences record the world as recognizable sensory patterns.***

These bits of sensory input organize to form patterns that lead to more complex integration of meanings. For example, if Mom uses sign language to communicate with her baby, the baby learns that the hand movements the baby sees mean something about a "dog," for example. The baby connects Mom's hand movement of tapping her thigh with the dog coming to Mom. By 6 months, the baby has usually learned enough meaning from recognizing the movement of Mom's hands matched with the dog that the baby is able to produce a hand sign to indicate "dog."

This is why babies can learn American Sign Language (ASL) at an early age. Use of ASL represents the baby's ability to imitate visual patterns that represent the underlying meaning of relationships the baby knows about the people, their actions, and their objects in the baby's world. However, the ability to make sounds to represent what the baby sees takes longer to develop, so a baby may not produce the first acoustic patterns of an utterance, "mama," until around 9 to 12 months of age.

Activity: Sensory input forms patterns from what types of experiences?

Babies require about 18-24 months of experiencing sensory patterns before they can use their hands or voices to indicate many relationships of meaning. These relationships are among the people (agents), their actions, and objects within the child's environment. For example, the parent calls the dog over, and the 18-month-old squats up and down squealing, "puppy, puppy, puppy!" This jumping up and down shows a movement or motor response to the incoming bits of information that the child has learned as part of her cognitive knowledge. The sound pattern of "puppy" is also a movement of the mouth or motor response to what the child knows. The child knows that these sound patterns, "puppy," connect to what the child sees and hears or knows about the dog. This state of early knowledge or cognitive development is grounded in sensory meanings.

Parents and educators watch what a child does in response to these sensory meanings and, in turn, assign meaning to the child's acts. The baby's or child's movements represent underlying cognitive development of the sensory learning. The caregiver assigns society's meaning to the child's actions. This stage is often called sensori-motor thinking or cognition (see Figure 1.5) (e.g., Piaget used the term "sensori-motor" to refer to the developmental period when an infant acts through the motor system to the sensory input) since it is based on a child responding to the sensory input with motor acts that caregivers use to assign meaning.

Activity: What is the earliest stage of cognitive development?

A child whose cognition is typical of this sensori-motor level does not recognize the meaning of ideas embedded in a picture or photograph. In other words, a sensori-motor level of development necessitates meaning through experiences of agents, actions, objects – not pictures. (More about using pictures with children severely impacted by autism and functioning at the sensori-motor level will be provided in Chapter 4.)

Sometimes professionals try to use pictures to teach concepts to a child who functions at this sensori-motor stage of development. If the child does not show an understanding of environmental events non-verbally – by pointing, gesturing, and/or verbally indicating relationships – the child does not have the cognitive development to see the meaning of what is in the pictures. Since the child at this level cannot see the relationships within a picture, using pictures at this level results in conditioning the child to respond to the pictures, rather than to what the child knows about the pictures. At this sensori-motor level, a child learns to respond in specific ways to pictures based on the patterns taught by adults. In other words, children from about 12-24 months can learn to recognize and demonstrate trained patterns in response to pictures shown over and over.

When these showings are paired with spoken patterns, many children are able to imitate and produce those spoken patterns to the pictures. For example, children turn the pages of a favorite book and say patterns, "dog," "cat," and so on. They may do the same with photo albums. Some children even do this patterning with entire sentences. For example, many young children repeat the nonsense rhyming of Dr. Seuss books – the acoustic patterns activate the children's brains! This activation assists the child in "wanting" to do the task over and over, thereby satisfying the brain's desire for more patterns. The brain only uses patterns at the lowest level of cognition.

With sufficient overlap between meaningful patterns that relate, a child will begin to show nonverbal understanding of cognitive relationships, such as who does what to whom – agent, action, object. Finally, the child is able to assign meaning to these semantic relationships with language patterns that represent the child's underlying development of concepts. At this level, the child is able to do more than just respond to patterns; the child is able to think in concepts.

Activity: What is the difference between learning patterns and concepts?

The ability to use pictures parallels the child's cognitive development. The child first sees nothing. Then he sees pieces of recognizable patterns, followed by seeing the relationships. And finally, the child sees the actual agents, actions, and objects within the picture.

Activity: The use of pictures parallels cognitive development. What is the hierarchy of using pictures – what does the child see first, second, and so forth?

The brain, neurologically, only uses patterns. For individuals with typical neurology, these patterns form concepts. But children with autism spectrum disorders (ASD) are not always able to develop patterns into concepts (Arwood & Kaulitz, 2007). For example, if the incoming sound patterns do not form spoken concepts, the child's imitation of the adult's sound system is purely a set of acoustic, non-meaningful patterns. The child is echoing the adult patterns.

Teaching a child to say an acoustic pattern in response to a picture or a series of pictures may result in helping the child learn to imitate the patterns, "green dog," "blue tree." The child's ability to imitate these patterns is in lieu of being able to learn and use concepts. ***In order for neurobiological sensory patterns to become concepts, the child must have a neurobiological system that converts the patterns into concepts.***

Activity: Why does the brain like to use patterns?

The child who is able to change the patterns into concepts is able to use the concepts in other situations, in novel ways, connected to nonverbal relationships among people, actions, and objects. For example, some children with early language development point to the neighbor's cat and say "dog?" and then look to the parent for a correction or clarification. Looking at the parent signals the parent to add meaning. When the child looks to the parent, the child is waiting for a response. This means that the child is able to recognize that the oral patterns of the parent's language connects or relates to the nonverbal concepts of what the child sees and knows.

The child "knows" the parent is an agent to the child, and the parent's actions (look, wait, speak) relate to what the child (agent) sees, hears, says, and so on. Most children with ASD pick up lots of different patterns very easily but are not always able to convert them into concepts. For example, some children with autism may be able to name 100 pictures, but never ask for help with a leaky glass or use gaze to signal another person to help with the leaking of the glass. Or they may be able to call out the alphabet, stack cups, or say borrowed sentences, but may not know when it is their turn to speak without interrupting.

Activity: What does a child with sensori-motor cognition "know"?

Children at the sensori-motor level of development possess a cognitive development that is sensory in nature with motor acts in response. This means that most visuals for a child of this age, or for this level of development of an older child who is severely impacted by autism, must be based on activities of the environment. The everyday activities create patterns, and the pictures of those everyday patterns offer a set of visual concepts for the child. Other types of pictures at this level of development have little meaning to a child. If a child can talk, read, or write about a picture's content, the child is functioning at a higher level. Since a child at this age does not typically read, write, or talk in elaborated forms, the pictures mean only what the child is able to see from experiences that match the pictures.

Since a child at the sensori-motor level of development has little conceptual development, pictures that are *not* about the child and what the child does in the child's world (the child is the agent performing actions with objects) have little meaning to the child. Children at the sensori-motor level must have visuals that match what they see in their environment.

Activity: What is the motor part of the sensori-motor stage of cognitive development?

Pictures at this age and level of sensori-motor development must relate to the meaning of physical experiences. When a child moves through space at this stage or looks at a visual, the child is an extension of what he can physically see, hear, or do. For example, if a child at this age looks at a picture, he will point to recognizable patterns of shape and meaning. Figure 3.1 shows a stick figure of a child looking at an *APRICOT I*[2] picture. The child points to parts of the picture and says "mama," "dog," "baby."

---

[2]   Arwood, E. (1985). *APRICOT I MANUAL and 50 Pictures*. Portland, OR: APRICOT Inc. This is a set of pictures and a manual. The pictures are 50 numbered and colored 8-1/2 by 11 inch lithographs designed to provide contexts for children to develop language.

Figure 3.1. Child sees herself looking at the pieces of a picture.

From Arwood, E. (1985). *APRICOT I MANUAL and 50 Pictures*. Picture #29. Portland, OR: APRICOT Inc. Used with permission.

The child is literally drawn into the picture she sees herself pointing to the picture. Until the child can see herself, she will not be able to extract any "conceptual" meaning from the task of looking at pictures. In other words, this type of picture is used to help the child learn about her own actions. The child at the lowest sensori-motor stage of development needs the real-life patterns of meaningful experiences connected between the child and any visuals used with the child.

The Language of Pictures for a child at the sensori-motor stage must connect to relationships about real-life experiences in the child's immediate world. In this case, the child is asked to look at pictures, so the educator draws the child looking at the picture the child will use in therapy. As the child begins to see him or herself in these pictures at this level, the child can begin to use pictures that are about others and their experiences. For example, a child must be able to sit and see "himself" sitting in a picture, performing an activity, before he can perceive others doing the same activity. Likewise, before a child is asked to look at a picture of a dog, the child has to be able to see the relationship between the child (agent) looking at the picture of the dog and the content of the picture, the dog.

In Figure 3.1, the child is drawn into the picture looking at the relationships among the mama (like the child's mama), a dog, and a baby. The child is not naming or labeling the objects or people in the picture; the child is pointing out the relationships among agents, actions, and objects. These relationships among patterns occur before the child is able to develop the stand-alone words for concepts.

Activity: What type of pictures works best for a child who functions at the early level of sensori-motor development?

Providing the child with photographs of the child engaged in activities does not do a better job of connecting the child to her sensori-motor knowledge of her world than drawing a picture of the child doing an activity. This does not mean that pictures cannot be used for children functioning at the sensori-motor level of development. It means that how the picture is used and when the picture is used in relationship to real-life experiences is critical. ***If a visual, such as a picture, is to have language meaning*** *for the child at this lowest sensori-motor stage of cognitive development, the picture must be a drawing of the child doing an act* (lowest level, Figure 3.1).

Figure 3.2a shows an adult drawing a child, hand-over-hand, into his picture of doing on a task. The child is literally a part of doing what he sees in the picture.

Figure 3.2a. **The child sees what he does.**

In Figure 3.2b, the picture requires more cognition than the one in 3.2a. First of all, Bobby is a floating head, not a whole person, so the child must use mental language or cognition to fill in the missing elements of the picture so as to recognize the head as a person. Second, the picture of Bobby does not look like the child who is looking at the picture, so who is this? Figure 3.2b requires more language for the child to be able to understand than Figure 3.2a, which had more information in the drawing.

Figure 3.2b. **A floating head.**

Activity: Why does Figure 3.2a require the child to use less language than Figure 3.2b to be able to see what the drawing is about?

Please note that the ages provided in this chapter relate to neurotypical learning, not necessarily the chronological age of a person with ASD. A person severely or profoundly impacted by autism may function at the sensori-motor age level as an adult, so the implications about using visuals remain the same. That is, if the person is functioning in response to sensory and perceptual patterns, he needs visuals that help develop his sense of agency. The person with sensori-motor development needs visuals that are of the impacted person (agent) doing what he can physically see and do (actions). More about the use of visuals at this level will be provided in later chapters.

At about 18 to 24 months of development (end of sensori-motor stage), the child begins nonverbally to act on agents, actions, and objects. For example, a child points to a dog, says "dog," looks up at Mom, who says, "Yes, that is a dog," and the child says, "Go dog, go!" At this age, the child is starting to move out of sensori-motor cognitive development and into more conceptual development about the child in relationship to other agents (people), their actions, and their objects. The child is beginning to show the meaning of the next level of language development, which represents the child's underlying socio-cognitive learning, "seeing others as part of his or her picture."

Activity: What does Stage One, a person at the sensori-motor level of learning, require in terms of the Language of Pictures?

Seeing Me - Stage Two of the Language Level of Pictures

At around 2 years of age, babies become much more mobile. Such mobility allows the child to act as an agent, a person who acts on others and their objects. This increase in agency allows the child to make the many cognitive connections between what the child does and what others do with, and for, the child. This is a significant time of developing one's self (Arwood & Young, 2000). The typical oral declaration, "Me do it," often accompanied by a nonverbal stomp, suggests to the adult that the child's meaning of his world relates to him and what he can do. Often this type of thinking operates on what the child knows, not what others in the world know.

The child's language learning continues at this stage until about age 7. Knowledge at this age, 2 to 7, is limited to the child knowing about his world in relationship to himself. Thus, the child's world is his world. Everything relates to the child! The child is central to others being in his picture. However, remember that in the first stage of verbal conceptual meaning, the child did not see others in a picture. Now, around age 2 to 3, the child is able to see himself in the picture in relationship to others.

With the child learning to be an agent who acts on and with others, the child is also learning that the world revolves around him so that he is central to *all* pictures. This means that if pictures are used with the child at this second level, the picture must show the child who is looking at the picture in order for the child to understand the meaning of others and their actions in the picture.

Activity: In addition to the child, who else does the child see in a picture at Stage Two of the Language of Pictures?

When a child at this stage looks at a picture that contains "strangers," she often labels one of the people as herself or others closely related to her, such as brothers, sisters, or classmates. She will name the people in the picture starting with her own name and the names of others she knows, even if the people in the picture are not really the child or her siblings.

The child is able to see the world from only her own perception and, therefore, does not operate according to what others do in relationship to the child. She does not see that the picture is about somebody else's class or family. Because the child operates on the meaning of her world from her own perspective, this stage of cognitive development is referred to as the *preoperational stage of cognitive development.*

Activity: What is the second stage of cognitive development?

It is at this preoperational stage of cognitive development that Language for Pictures begins to represent more than just patterns or basic relationships among patterns. A child in Stage Two begins to use his underlying knowledge as a reference point for others' actions. The child begins to see others act within his own context. The child expects others to "do" for the child, because the child is there! The child expects others to meet his needs – whatever the child wants and whenever the child needs what he wants. The world revolves around what the child knows – him or herself. The child is the center of the universe.

It should be noted that even though this stage is supposed to be finished by age 7, children with developmental disabilities, such as those impacted by ASD, may be much older but still functioning at this level of conceptual development.

Activity: What are some of the characteristics of the preoperational stage of cognitive development?

Since a preoperational child shows conceptual meaning about himself to others and to the world, the Language of Pictures relates also to the child and to the child's world. For example, a simple black-and-white drawn cartoon frame labeling what the child does in the child's world has more meaning at this stage than a pretty, commercial picture of a child that the adult labels as the child. Figures 3.2a and 3.2b showed these comparisons. Figure 3.2a showed the adult hand-over-hand drawing the child, Bobby, into looking at a picture – in this way the child sees himself looking at the picture of a book. Figure 3.2b was of someone else without the child in the picture.

Language at this preoperational stage represents what a child knows in relationship to himself.
Language at this stage begins to function as a tool for acquiring more meaning about the early concepts of agents, actions, and objects in relationship to the child. A child's true connection between oral language and underlying conceptual development begins with this second stage. The child at this preoperational stage of language sees himself in a picture that someone else labels. The child may or may not see the meaning of other objects in the picture or actions in the picture, depending on what the child knows conceptually about those meanings. Figure 3.3 shows a black-and-white scan of an APRICOT I colored picture.

Figure 3.3. **Picture #47, Raking Leaves.**
From Arwood, E. (1985). *APRICOT I MANUAL and 50 Pictures.* Picture #47. Portland, OR: APRICOT Inc. Used with permission.

However, a particular 6-year-old child, Emma, diagnosed with an ASD was not in the picture; therefore, she could not see the meaning of the whole picture. Emma looked at the picture and pointed to a girl in the picture. Emma then talked about what she did at school. Emma insisted that the picture was about what her friend at school did that was wrong, borrowing spoken patterns she heard her teacher say such as "Bad boys are not nice."

The adult working with Emma could not redirect her, by using language or by pointing, to the real meaning of the picture. Finally, the adult redrew the story into multiple overlapping relationships. Only when this child could see all of the different meaningful relationships among the agents, actions, and objects did she begin to understand the whole picture.

Figure 3.4 shows how the educator drew with paper and pencil all of the relationships in order to create a whole picture of conceptual meaning for the child. They worked through each picture of all the frames in Figure 3.4 to develop enough conceptual meaning for Emma to be able to "see" the meaning of the original picture.

***Figure 3.4*. Raking the leaves as nine connected pictures.**

From Arwood, E., & Brown, M. (1999). *A guide to cartooning and flowcharting* (p. 32). Portland, OR: APRICOT Inc. Used with permission.

By connecting the meaning of the agents, actions, and objects through several pictures, the child could begin to see the agents, actions, and objects as concepts within pictures.

Even though this typically talkative child appeared to have a lot of spoken language, Emma did not have the underlying concepts of what her oral patterns meant. As a result of the lack of meaning, she had severe behavior issues. She did not understand the words that others used in seeking compliance. When the adult drew out the ideas within a story picture into multiple pictures of agents, actions, and objects, this young child began to *see* the meaning of the world around her and to understand the meaning of others' spoken words connected to her actions or behaviors. Her behavior changed dramatically, and the changes paralleled her ability to see what was in the picture. In other words, as she became able to recognize more of the relationships in the picture, this cognitive ability helped her to begin to see more relationships between her behavior and the actions of others in her environment.

Similar use of drawings of her environment helped this child learn the meaning of concepts such as "get ready" or "clean up." In nine months, she moved from a child who was behaviorally out of control, even though she had received three years of discrete behavior trial therapy, to a child who understood enough about how to make her body match the meaning of the pictures so that she was included in a general education classroom. Her conceptualization of language patterns helped her learn the concepts of the patterns of what others said as well as what she said herself. The pictures were drawn to match her developmental level of language. The content of the pictures provided her with the conceptual meaning of her immediate world so that she could turn the patterns of speech into the meaning of language.

Activity: How do the multiple pictures of Figure 3.4 help a child see the meaning of concepts in one picture?

The basic relationships among concepts of agents, their actions, and their objects, as they connect to each other and to the child, are the foundation to learning language.

The use of developmentally appropriate visuals for a child who is at the preoperational stage must relate the child to the use of agents, actions, and objects in the child's environment. From these types of visuals, the preoperational child can begin to learn the concepts of the picture and relate the language to the meaning of the picture. The more language the child develops about the basic relational concepts, the more meaning she is able to bring to a visual.

Because the preoperational level of development is *all* about the child, a child at this age or stage needs pictures that show the relationships of the child's environment. Figure 3.5 is an APRICOT I picture designed to provide the relationships among people or agents, actions, and objects in a location that is all on one plane. In this way, multiple sets of basic semantic relationships (agents to actions to objects) are tied together in context of a story to provide the meaning to the language of the story. A picture that lacks the meaning of these types of relationships will not help a child at this level develop her understanding of her own environment. (Additional information about how to choose visuals will be provided in later chapters.)

Figure 3.5. **Picture #4, The Grocery Store Display.**

From Arwood, E. (1985), *APRICOT I MANUAL and 50 Pictures.* Picture #4. Portland, OR: APRICOT, Inc. Used with permission.

Figure 3.6 shows an iconic[3] picture of an object, a ball.

Figure 3.6. **Photo of an object.**

As an adult, the reader recognizes the object separate from meaningful relationships of the object, ball. The adult reader is able to use language to connect the picture to what the adult knows about a ball – throw a ball, bat a ball, play with a ball in the park, attend a professional baseball game, and so on. The more language the adult has developed, the more information about the picture the adult can use to recognize the meaning of the photograph.

---

3   Iconic pictures are drawings representative of what the real item looks like. For example, a young child draws what looks like a tree. The child's drawing is iconic. Symbolic pictures represent a whole set of activities such as a single toilet representing the many activities involved in toileting, such as walking to the bathroom, walking to the toilet, pulling down pants, etc.

A child at the preoperational stage of cognition may not be able to see the photographed object because there are no connections or relationships to help decipher the meaning of the object in the photograph. In other words, the preoperational child may not have enough language to be able to recognize the object in the picture without additional meaning from relationships of the object to the people or agents using the object. Furthermore, the child is not in the picture, which makes seeing the object in relationship to a preoperational thinker very difficult.

In order for a child to "see" the single object in a photograph, the child must be able to bring his ideas about the object to the picture. A child can be conditioned to recognize the patterns of the picture and say the pattern given to imitate. For example, a photograph of ball is presented to the child, and the adult says "ball" for the child to imitate. The child is reinforced for responding. Eventually, the child is shown a random assortment of pictured objects at which the child looks and says imitated vocal patterns. However, without the concept of what the pictured object means, the child does not use the pattern meaningfully because he does not have the patterns as concepts.

For example, the child is told to go pick up the ball or to toss the ball but does not respond. The adult hands the child the real ball and says, "What's this?" Again, the child does not respond. In order for the child to have conceptual meaning about a visual at the preoperational level of meaning, she needs the Language of the Picture, which means that she needs to "know" what the object means in terms of basic semantic relationships among agents, actions, and objects.

Labeling of real objects such as "This is a ball" or "What is this?" is also a pattern, not the development of relationships of agents, actions, and objects. Remember: ***The semantic relationships among agents, actions, and objects form the basis of language and the foundation to preoperational thinking!***

When given a picture without agents, actions, and objects, some children do not recognize the patterns of any object and, therefore, see nothing in the picture but shades of gray. If the goal of using a picture is to help a child learn cognitively and socially, the Language of Pictures must match the child's level of cognition.

Activity: Why does a single-object picture make interpretation of the meaning of the picture more difficult for a child?

Figure 3.7 shows how a ball is an object within the environment that the child knows. This picture is easier to interpret than the one in Figure 3.6 for a child who is at a preoperational stage of language learning. This is because the picture in Figure 3.7 provides more meaning about the object in relationship to others, which gives more meaning to the object as a concept.

Figure 3.7. **Picture #12, Playing Basketball.**

From Arwood, E. (1985), *APRICOT I MANUAL and 50 Pictures.* Picture #12. Portland, OR: APRICOT, Inc. Used with permission

The APRICOT I pictures used in Figures 3.5 and 3.7 are examples of the type of pictures that provide a preoperational level of language. Both pictures show children or agents doing something that most children with preoperational thinking can identify with. Both pictures show the basic relationships among agents, actions, and objects. A child who is at this language level needs pictures that show the child how he fits into the meaning of his environment. The more relational meaning there is within a picture, the easier the picture is for the child to interpret. Both types of pictures are easier for a preoperationally thinking child than the single-object type of picture in Figure 3.2b or Figure 3.6.

The Language of Pictures for Figures 3.5 or 3.7 is easier because the child does not need to infer the meaning of missing information such as what is this object (ball) used for and with whom and why and when, and so on. The visible relationships within the pictures in Figures 3.5 and 3.7 provide the information about agents, actions, and objects for the child. This information gives the child more meaning about concepts the child is acquiring. In other words, the pictures in Figures 3.5 and 3.7 provide more language for the child, resulting in the child not needing as much language to interpret the meaning of the picture.

Activity: What types of information should a picture for preoperational thinkers provide?

Most individuals who are diagnosed with an ASD function in some areas of their lives at the preoperational level, whether it is for the learning of oral language, learning of social skills, the refinement of more advanced concepts such as "forestry," or learning how to manage time. Later chapters will discuss this preoperational level of the Language of Pictures with additional examples.

Seeing Is Believing! – Stage Three of the Language Levels of Pictures

Once a child learns the relationships between herself and her environment (preoperational thinking), she begins to see others and what they do in their pictures separate from the child. This ability to see how others fit into her pictures allows a child to think about the relationship between her own actions and others' needs, actions, thoughts, feelings, and so forth. ***This solid or concrete level of cognitive operation allows the child to put others into the child's pictures of thinking as well as to begin to see others in pictures separate from the child.*** The Language of Pictures at this level shows what others do but may exclude the child from having to be in the picture. The child can see what others do in pictures where the child is no longer part of the picture.

The language at this stage is quite advanced. This stage begins at about 7 years of age for neurotypical learners and continues to refine conceptual knowledge until about 11 years of age. A neurotypical language learner has adult language structures at about 7 to 8 years of age and is able to carry on a two-way conversation with another person about whatever knowledge the two share. This advanced level of language means that pictures can be less relational because the person looking at the picture can fill in the missing relationships through language.

Activity: What defines Stage Three level of cognitive development?

Figure 3.8 shows a picture of children learning to take turns in order to play ball. Following rules about what others want and expect requires a concrete level of understanding or cognition.

Figure 3.8. **Children are learning to play ball.**

A child at this concrete level of language is able to take all of the language about what he knows about people, playing ball, taking turns, asking to play, and so on, and put it into knowledge or conceptual meaning about what he sees or perceives in a picture. This child is able to operate on the relationships of others.

For example, others create the classroom rules the child follows to be an agent with in the classroom. For a child to understand the classroom rules from the adult's perspective, the child must be at this concrete level. The adult tells a high school student that he is to call all adults by their last name with title such as Ms.

Glenn or Mr. James. This high school student, who is on the autism spectrum, begins a long process of inquiry in an attempt to understand the rules: "Why do I have to call them by their last names?"

No matter how many explanations of authority, and so on, he received, he continued with the "name game" rules every time he met a person, and sometimes with people he had known for a long time. He could repeat the rules, and he could usually follow the rules, but he did not understand the rules at the concrete level. He could not think about others without putting himself into the center of the picture.

Putting himself always back into the picture means he was functioning at the second stage of language – preoperational – not at a concrete, or Stage Three, level of development where he would need to be able to understand most rules. Finally, with much drawing at a lower or preoperational level with the written language to go with the drawings, he was able to see the rule without needing to put himself in every picture.

Understanding concrete rules is part of this stage of cognitive development because they are about other people and what other people need. Children or adults will only understand the concrete concepts *if* they have the language for the meaning of the concepts.

Activity: Why does an understanding of rules involve other people?

Figure 3.9 shows an individual picture separate from any meaningful relationship to an object. This picture conceptually works for children who are concrete or formal in their thinking and, therefore, have lots of adult structures of language. But the response of a child at a lower level of language development does not represent conceptual knowledge.

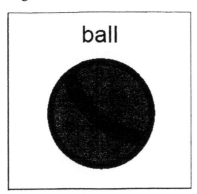

Figure 3.9. **Ball.**

A child who does not have the language concepts but is able to "cue" off or "respond" to a single-object picture gives a pattern of response, not a conceptual response. Since single-object types of pictures "symbolize" underlying concepts, they are much more difficult to interpret. If a child is learning a new concept, she must bring a lot more language to symbols than to the preoperational pictures of events. Events connect people, their actions, and objects into a meaningful context. When a person is looking at a picture that has a lot of missing or incomplete "symbolized" information, he must bring a lot of language to the picture to create the underlying, missing, meaning of the concepts.

In addition to symbolized objects, other types of pictures are also concrete or higher. Figure 3.10 is about people doing lots of different actions. Not everyone is on the same plane with the same perspective. Therefore, this picture requires the learner to bring enough language to make the connections about the people who are doing different actions. Understanding multiple people doing a variety of things, not in relationship to each other, requires concrete or higher language.

Figure 3.10. **Concrete camping.**

In contrast to the concrete picture about camping, Figure 3.11 shows a preoperational picture of camping.

Figure 3.11. **Picture #20, The Camp.**

From Arwood, E. (1985). *APRICOT I MANUAL and 50 Pictures.* Picture #20. Portland, OR: APRICOT, Inc. Used with permission.

In the preoperational picture about camping (Figure 3.11), the campers are drawn doing their actions on the same plane. Their arms, legs, hands, and faces are visible. They are all involved in the same event. Therefore, the learner who looks at this picture does not have to bring as much information or language to the picture as would have to bring to the picture in Figure 3.10.

Figure 3.12 is more difficult than a preoperational level. It has a social context that requires problem solving. Social problem solving is a form of critical thinking, which is at the concrete level or higher. In other words, Figures 3.10 and 3.12 are both concrete, or higher, levels of pictures, but 3.12 is more difficult than Figure 3.10 because of the added social problem. Figures 3.10 and 3.12 require more cognition and language than the preoperational, event-based picture in Figure 3.11.

Figure 3.12. **Picture #9, The Fall.**

From Arwood, E. (1989). *APRICOT II MANUAL.* Picture #9.[4] Portland, OR: APRICOT, Inc. Used with permission.

This picture is about individuals involved in a social context that requires an understanding of the basic semantic relationships of others as well as the expected societal rules. The child's ability to see all of these relationships and the social rules that go with the pictured situation is at a concrete language level. Many adolescents or adults who have lower levels of meaning look at this picture and drop back to almost a sensory level. They label pieces of the picture because they cannot see the bigger concepts.

When learners cannot see the meaning of the overall picture, they produce the bits they are able to see. For example, a 15-year-old who appeared to be functioning at a higher level of language looked at the picture and said, "Boy falls." This picture is designed to represent multiple cognitive options. One possibility is that the man trips over the boy's bike. Another possibility is that the man trips over the boy's baseball equipment, or the man falls off the ladder. Even with questioning, this youth saw the person on the ground as a boy who had hurt his ankle. But he did not see the relationships among the bike on the grass and the person who tripped over the bike or the person who fell and the baseball equipment or the person who fell and the ladder. The picture is full of social language opportunities and multiple

---

4 APRICOT II is a kit of black-and-white pictures accompanied by a manual. Each picture is numbered and relates to a social problem.

ways to assign meaning. But this particular 15-year-old saw only one relationship, a boy is hurt because he fell, which suggests that he is responding at a preoperational, not a concrete, level to a concrete picture. He is thinking about himself falling.

To improve the teen's thinking, the picture in Figure 3.12 was broken into multiple stories consisting of multiple pictures so that he could see multiple social relationships among agents, their actions, and their objects, thereby increasing his language.

In summary, the third stage of the language levels of pictures is concrete and represents what a child or adult knows about what others do or act in their environment.

Activity: How is the third stage of concrete cognition different from the pre-operational or sensori-motor levels of cognition?

Symbols Only - Stage Four of the Language Levels of Pictures

The fourth stage of language for understanding what is in a picture is solely based on language symbols. That is, it is not predicated on the use of agents, actions, and objects, and the meaningful relationships among them. ***This fourth stage uses language to symbolize the meaning of what one perceives as knowledge.***

In Figure 3.12, the picture could be interpreted at a fourth or formal stage of development. "The boy, in the baseball outfit, saw the man who was painting the house fall off the ladder, so the boy dropped his baseball equipment and jumped off his bike to help him. In this way, the boy is being considerate of the needs of the man who is hurt. On the other hand, when the man fell, he broke the awning, so he accepts responsibility for repairing the awning, if he is a considerate worker." Formal concepts like "considerate" and "responsible" symbolize many concepts tied together in related meanings.

The statement, liberty is justice, does not represent something that a learner can touch, smell, taste, hear, or see. The ideas within the statement combine to mean something greater than the individual concepts or patterns of the spoken or printed words. If a person were to picture the ideas that would connect or represent the meaning of this statement, he would mentally see multiple pictures, perhaps even a mental movie clip. Adults who work with mental language, either in visual graphics or words or the mental sound of their own voices, use symbolic language to represent formal concepts. This formal way of using language is cognitively separate from any iconic image of a graphic or drawing.

Even though formal concepts are not based in physical sensory experience, many adults try to teach these complex concepts with a single picture or with a single set of skills or rules. For example, most schools have positive behavior supports (PBS) about how to be considerate, respectful, empathetic, courteous, and so forth. These concepts are formal, abstract concepts that require a lot of language to understand. In order for a child to understand a formal concept such as "Be considerate!," she needs to be able to see what those words, "Be considerate," *look like* when agents, their actions, and objects represent the meaning of those formal words. A child will not understand the language of "Be considerate" without first seeing the mental visuals depicted in multiple settings. Even a child at the concrete level of language will struggle with what it means to "Be considerate" unless she has the meaning at a preoperational level.

To acquire the formal meaning of the rule "to be considerate," the child must acquire the meaning of multiple examples of what "to be considerate" looks like. In other words, the child needs to "see" many different instances of people "being considerate" and be able to talk, read, write, listen, and think about how each instance is an example of what it means "to be considerate." Since the concept of what it means "to be considerate" is the most abstract and therefore formal, the meaning of "to be considerate" must be distinctive from other formal concepts such as "to be respectful." "To be considerate" is similar to the meaning of the concept "to be respectful" because many of the same examples could be used for both concepts, but there is a slight difference. When a child understands these slight differences in the meaning of these formal concepts, the child is functioning at a formal level of understanding. More about formal types of pictures will be offered in later chapters.

Activity: What is the fourth stage of cognitive development of the Language of Pictures?

If the child's level of understanding the meaning of the Language of Pictures does not match the level of language of a picture given the child to learn a concept, skill, or language task, learning will be limited.

Summary

There are four stages of cognitive development parallel to the acquisition of the meaning of the Language of Pictures. Using pictures to help develop the Language of Pictures requires that the pictures match the child's cognitive thinking. The more meaning a picture has that relates to the child, the less language the child has to bring to the picture. Therefore, pictures with more agents, actions, and objects are easier for a child to understand and use for learning than pictures that lack agents, actions, and objects.

Very low-functioning children can use pictures for learning if they are literally drawn into the pictures so that the picture matches what they are doing. Higher-order thinkers are able to gradually use fewer and fewer details within pictures because they have more language. But if a learner does not have much meaning about a concept, pictures that match the learner's lower level of thinking must be used.

Pictures of objects or people do not provide much meaning and, therefore, can result in a child responding to them in a conditioned response format, rather than from a conceptual viewpoint. When the child does not use concepts for perceiving the meaning of a visual, the visual does not provide much language or cognitive development. Therefore, the child will stay at the language or cognitive level that he already uses. However, pictures that match a child's cognitive level can be arranged to plan a child's increase in language and cognitive development. Chapter 4 will discuss how to select pictures for academic purposes.

CHAPTER 4

Selecting Visuals for Academic Use

I see what I know,

I understand what I see ...

But I know only what my language sees.

The journey of understanding the Language of Pictures began in the first chapter with an explanation of how visuals represent personal meaning. Chapter 2 described how different people perceive different meanings to the same picture. Chapter 3 provided a description of the cognitive levels of language for the various pictures. This chapter describes how to select visuals based on the child's language level.

Language Development

When a child looks at a picture or any other type of visual, she is able to construct meaning about the picture according to her level of language development. So, a child thinks about what she understands in the picture or visual. For example, if a child enjoys and celebrates knowing the names of various dinosaurs, the child is able to see and name a picture of a dinosaur that she knows. But if the same capable child looks at a picture of a galaxy in an adult-type of science magazine, she may not respond.

It is possible that the child not only does not recognize any meaning in the galaxy picture, the child may not see anything on the page. In other words, the child may think the page of the galaxy picture is blank. Without language for a concept like "galaxy," the child does not see anything on the page. To be able to see the meaning in a picture or to interpret the meaning of a picture, the child uses the language at her current stage of development.

The Language of Pictures comes in part from a child's language ability. As a child acquires conceptual meaning, the child's language ability increases (see Chapter 2 for an explanation of how a child acquires meaning and Chapter 3 for the parallel cognitive stages of meaning). The more meaning a child acquires, the more meaning he brings to looking at a visual. When a child looks at a picture or visual, he brings his language meaning to the picture. ***The more meaning a child brings to a picture through language, the less meaning the visual needs to depict.***

For example, if a child has lots of meaning about lions, he immediately recognizes a picture of a lion, whether the lion's whole body is visible or not. If the child does not have sufficient meaning to recognize an incomplete picture of a lion (Figure 4.1), he will need to see more characteristics of the concepts surrounding a lion to be able to recognize the meaning of the picture of the lion.

***Figure 4.1.* A lion's face.**
Adapted with permission from a photograph by Edmond Y. Young, Portland, Oregon.

Surrounding concepts might include the whole lion, background grass, sky, and so on. The more advanced the child's language development is, the less the picture has to show about the topic. Children who have little language development need more contextual meaning to be able to see what is in a picture. For example, a child who does not know a lot about lions may need to see the whole lion's body, including four feet and a tail, as well as the lion's living environment to recognize that the picture is of a lion (see Figure 4.2).

***Figure 4.2.* A lion in his natural setting.**
Photograph published with permission, Edmond Y. Young, Portland, Oregon.

> *Activity: Why does a child with less language need more context to be able to meaningfully use a picture?*

The language of the child represents what the child knows. What a child knows is the child's level of conceptualization. Concept acquisition occurs through multiple overlapping sensory inputs or experiences within a context. The child's experience consists of the sensory input from the context. For example, a child may be able to label a picture of a lion from practicing what to say when the adult shows the picture. But for the child to explain how a lion is different from a tiger and how a tiger is different from a zebra, the child would need a lot more information about a tiger in relationship to a lion and about a tiger in contrast and comparison to a zebra. This extra information is part of the experience surrounding a concept. **The surrounding, related information of a concept is called the context. Context provides information about the relationships of concepts.** With context, a child can learn how one idea or concept differs from another idea or concept.

Without context, acquisition of the meaning of concepts is restricted. **If concept acquisition is restricted, language development is also restricted.** How much language a child brings to a visual graphic or picture depends on the child's language development level, which represents the child's acquisition of concepts. So, **how well a child is able to learn from a visual or to use a visual for communication depends on the child's language development.** Different children have different levels of language development; therefore, different children need different types of visuals.

> *Activity: Why do different children need different visuals?*

When selecting visuals for a child, knowing the child's language development level helps the parent or educator select visuals that match the child's level of conceptual or language learning. The better the match between the child's level of language and the difficulty level of the language of the picture, the more effective is the use of visuals or pictures for intervention. How much language is in a picture matched to what a child knows about the language of the picture determines what the child is able to "see" or recognize in the picture.

> *Activity: Why does knowing a child's language level help in providing education to a child?*

The Language of a Picture

There are several meaning acquisition levels in a child's development (Arwood's Neurosemantic Language Learning Theory; see Chapters 2 and 3). The first level of meaning is sensory, or the physical input of what a person hears or sees. These features of sensory input overlap to form perceptions of what a child hears, sees, tastes, touches, and so on. The second level of patterns of input creates concepts, *if* the patterns are the same type of patterns that the child's neurobiological system is able to use for developing concepts.

Concept development is the third level of meaning. Remember that not all children use the same types of patterns to form concepts. Children and adults diagnosed with autism spectrum disorders (ASD) typically use visual patterns developed from the shapes of movements (motor planning), such as the movement of the mouth, movement of the hands, and so forth (Arwood & Kaulitz, 2007). The language concepts for a person with ASD are visual in nature. Therefore, the use of pictures is important for a person with ASD; but the person with ASD also needs the language of the picture to be able to use the visual effectively. ***Language, the fourth level of meaning or neurosemantics, represents a person's level of conceptual development.***

Activity: What are the four levels of meaning in Arwood's Neurosemantic Language Learning Theory?

When considering the language of a picture, it is important to ask, "How much meaning or language does the child possess about the picture or visual?" – "What is the child's functional language level?"

Beginning to See "What" Is in a Picture

Since the eyes record absence or presence of light, it is important to present a child with very low acquisition of concepts visual patterns that show the contrast between light and dark. A dark pencil mark on white paper provides more contrast than filled-in or shaded figures. In other words, physically, the eyes can see the black pencil lines on the white contrast of paper better than they can see the shades of colors. Without conceptual meaning of colors, a child's eyes see shades that are relative to each other, not to the words denoting color such as red, blue, and so on. Black on white provides the most contrast and works best for individuals with the lowest level of language.

Pencil line drawings on white paper also provide more white space between the images or concepts on the paper. This means that it is easier to see the lines of the image of a person than complete bodies shaded in. Figure 4.3 is easier to physically see than Figure 4.4.

Figure 4.3. Cartoon of broken boat picture.

Figure 4.4. **Black-and-white version of Picture #39, The Broken Boat.**

This book is using back-and-white scans of the APRICOT I pictures. The original APRICOT I pictures are colored, which helps provide meaning for some students, but at the same time the color makes seeing the relationships difficult for lower functioning children. The relational drawing in Figure 4.3, which is a black-and-white drawing, is easier than the colored (or black and white) version of the APRICOT I picture in Figure 4.4. The black-on-white contrast drawing of specific people (agents), their actions, and their objects is much easier for a child to see.

As children develop more language for concepts, they are able to use color as meaningful information. In other words, color does not add conceptual meaning; it helps add perceptual layers of meaning to the concepts that the child already "knows." Therefore, a black-and-white line drawing of people or agents doing things is easier to understand than a colored picture.

Because children who lack a lot of visual mental language usually learn their visual mental concepts from shapes made through movements, drawing in real time makes the pictures in Figure 4.3 even easier to understand. As we have seen, the eyes record not just the absence or presence of light but move along with the body, recording the points of light that reflect off the edges of a body, object, or plane. In this way, it is often easier for a child to see movements than non-movements.

When black-on-white line drawings are created in real time, the eye can actually see the hand make movements that the child is able to see as a shape of the idea. The child may see the shapes of the movements of the pencil better than the finished drawn product. At this level of language development, the sensory input of light and movement creates meaning for the child. This is a very low level of developmental meaning and requires careful consideration of the visual materials to ensure they are effective for a given child.

Activity: Why does drawing a relational set of pictures like the cartoon in Figure 4.3 provide more information than an already prepared picture?

The meaning a child brings to a picture helps her understand the meaning of the picture. *When the child is recognizing the meaning of the contrast of light and movement, the child's understanding of the visual is at a sensori-motor to preoperational level of development* (see Chapter 3). This means that the content of the drawing has to be about him and his activities of daily living to create sufficient context for the child to understand the patterns on the paper. Pictures of objects that lack sufficient context or that are removed from the child and the child's immediate context do not provide enough meaning to help a child at this level acquire meaning for the relationships of the depicted objects.

Figure 4.5 shows a simple cartoon of a child walking into class and hanging up his coat.

Figure 4.5. **Getting started in the morning.**

This cartoon was first drawn in real time, which means the cartoon was drawn with the child watching. Then the adult assisted the child in physically moving through the act of walking into class and hanging up his coat. Educators hung these pictures along with many other conceptual picture cartoons around the room. In this way, the child began to see himself do the various tasks during the day. He is in the pictures of concepts that he learns. The pictures show him in his immediate context.

The written words were then added to the picture concepts to help the student see the overlap between what he does (picture) and what he sees written. Providing the written words with the pictures enabled the child to see the visual-motor patterns of the writing matching the concepts of the pictures. In this way, the patterns and concepts combined to form the language of the pictures. ***These types of pictures not only resulted in quick compliance in terms of behavior but also began to help the child learn to conceptualize his world.***

Activity: Why does drawing the cartoon with the child help the child see the contents of the cartoon better than presenting the child with prepared drawings?

For children with ASD who are beginning to develop the meaning of language and are, therefore, functioning at the sensori-motor level of development, high-contrast, black-and-white real-time drawings of the child in the child's immediate context provide the most appropriate level of meaning. These types of drawings help move the child to the next stage, the stage of preoperational thinking.

Activity: Why does real-time drawing help children see what is on the page?

Expanding on Seeing the Content of a Picture

Educators at the APRICOT Learning, Language, and Behavior Clinic in Tigard, Oregon, developed a protocol of what type of visual is appropriate for children at various levels of language and cognitive development. Table 4.1 shows a summary of the APRICOT protocol of language meaning of visuals at different levels of cognitive and language development.

Table 4.1

Summary of Language Meaning of Visuals at Different Levels of Cognitive and Language Development

Cognition	Language	Academics	Best Visual Type
Sensori-motor level of development	Child does not have oral language or imitates and echoes others	Child's academics are patterns; repeat stacking cups, naming colors, counting numbers	Draw pictures within and about activities of daily living; label all pictures with written words in context; use H/H [hand-over-hand] for pointing to elements of pictures and for executing
Preoperational level of cognitive development	Child is able to show understanding of agent, action, object relationships; may or may not have natural language	Child will use the writing to learn to read, speak, and increase cognitive development; writing is H/H and overlapped with other motor acts such as finger spelling, typing, ADLs [activities of daily living], mouth movements with no sound; all of these can be accomplished using H/H	Draw real-time cartoons with the child in the picture; use H/H for layers of motor acts, such as drawing for the child to learn to read, write, think, spell, etc.
Preoperational to concrete level of cognitive development	Child has some ability to use oral language; rules are restricted; misunderstands socials, directions, etc.	Child learns concepts from motor acts connected with writing and drawn concepts that the child can write and read	Use event-based pictures like APRICOT I pictures with cartoons of writing matched to pictures (see Figure 4.3)
Concrete cognitive development	Child has lots of language	Child struggles with inferred meanings or conceptual meanings of academics; some people see the child as smart and others question child's ability; child does academic patterns well but may not understand concrete rules and formal concepts	Begin new concepts with iconic drawings matched to written words and refine concepts with writing to drawings
Formal level of cognitive development	Child is at upper end of the spectrum for language; may need more social language and also may need refinement of concepts	Child produces the academic patterns very easily but may show problems with critical thinking that is socially appropriate	Use writing matched to drawings and words in diagrams, icons, PowerPoints, computer flowcharts, visual flowcharts

From Brown, M., & Arwood, E. (2007. November). *A therapeutic protocol for visual language meaning*. Presentation at Language Is Learning: The Metacognitive Basis to Symbolization and Semantic Memory, Portland, Oregon.

The content of Table 4.1 serves as a guide for which materials to use for assessment and intervention to improve cognition, language, and/or behavior. The chart is a guideline for acquisition of new concepts. When a child has a lot of meaning for a family of related concepts, such as dinosaurs, a higher level of pictures for that content may be appropriate. The less meaning the child has about the content meaning of a picture, the more the child needs context to go with the visuals.

The intervention rule of thumb is to begin at the child's level and increase the complexity of the task to the next level with the same content. In this way, the education begins at the child's conceptual language level. Be patient, and use the same content across levels of development, using multiple visuals for the same content. In this way, the child begins to acquire the concepts of the visuals.

For example, Johnny was an 8-year-old male who used no spontaneous speech and showed limited academic development. However, with the use of cartooning of what it looks like for Johnny to leave his home and come to the clinic to work, he has been able to come and work in the clinic. At the clinic, the educator uses pictures of people doing actions within a story context so that Johnny can see himself in the event. This type of picture was chosen since Johnny's understanding of his world (conceptual language) is at a preoperational level; the world is about him.

Johnny's learning system is dependent on him being able to see the shape of the educator's hand move in order for him to acquire concepts. So the educator uses multiple layers of movement to help Johnny acquire concepts. They hand-over-hand (H/H) write words to the picture, sign in his hand the finger spelling of the words, fingerspell and bubble write words on a picture dictionary page, sometimes finger spell the word on the table (no actual writing, just the movement), and sometimes show him the movement of the adult's face saying the concept of the ideas of the picture. They then H/H write the story, which is bubbled, and the educator points to the words as Johnny tries to say them.

This process can add more layers if needed. For Johnny to be able to learn concepts, the educator must begin with a visual picture that is at his level of thinking. Then the educator must teach him the concepts within the picture with what Johnny needs for learning. Johnny has now begun to read the stories that he wrote several months ago, showing that by beginning with a picture representative of his language level and adding layers to his knowledge through lots of meaning, he has begun to learn to read. He now has some speech and is also able to write concepts he knows.

The effectiveness of therapy with Johnny is a direct result of the many layers of visuals that have been used with him in his home, therapy, and work setting. The family and educator overlap meaning of visual concepts until Johnny shows a change in his behavior or academic learning.

Activity: Often intervention begins with a picture, the child responds, and then the educator starts another picture. Why would it be more effective to stay with the same content across multiple visual inputs?

As a child develops more meaning of concepts, she begins to read, write, and talk about her environment. Once the child is able to use language to talk, read, and write about the concepts, the language within the pictures provides more advanced levels of meaning. Visuals or pictures bring various levels of meaning to a child. The levels of meaning for a picture depend on what a child's brain is able to recognize. A child recognizes the meaning in the picture based on what she knows about the concepts in the picture and will be able to represent her knowledge of those concepts through language.

A picture that a child is able to use to help develop language is a picture that the child is able to recognize as meaningful. The use of pictures to teach concepts or language takes into consideration the context of the concepts being taught as well as the child's language level about the depicted concepts. For example, if a child is not toilet trained and does not show language development about toilet training, training a child to point to the picture of a toilet each time before he goes to the toilet teaches the child that the pictured is associated with going to the toilet. Figure 4.6 shows a single toileting picture.

***Figure 4.6.* Toilet.**

This single picture will not teach the child how to be independent in toileting, but it does provide a form of communication. When the child points to the toilet and is taken to the toilet, the assumption is that the child understands the meaning of the concepts related to toileting. Most children who need this level of communication also need to learn concepts so that they can develop language. ***Since language represents concepts, the child has to increase conceptualization if language is the desired outcome.***

Activity: What types of concepts does a child understand if he can point to a picture to represent multiple meanings?

For a child who needs to develop concepts in order to increase cognition and language, multiple pictures drawn in real time like those in Figures 4.7a and 4.7b are easier to understand than the single use of a symbolized concept. The pictures in Figures 4.7a and 4.7b are a set of pictures used with a preschooler to learn the process of toileting.

Figures 4.7a and 4.7b. **Using the bathroom.**

Drawn by Kitty Mulkey of Firestone, Colorado, for APRICOT, Inc., in 1995. Used with permission.

Selecting Visuals for Academic Use

Figures 4.7a and 4.7b show more meaning about toileting than a single picture. Because the cartoon has more context than a single picture, it provides more conceptual meaning. This cartoon is effective for a child who does not have the language for toileting. The multiple pictures provide the child with the language of toileting concepts. Furthermore, each act of the concepts about toileting is drawn for the child so he can see what he looks like going to the bathroom. In this way, the child learns the concepts of toileting, not just how to respond to a picture.

If more learning about a language concept such as toileting is desired, the pictures must show more context of how the concepts relate. In the case of toileting, the concepts include thinking about going to the bathroom, walking to the bathroom, the child pulling down his pants, the child sitting on the toilet, and so on. In this way, the meaning of "going to the bathroom" is depicted in the pictures so that the child can begin to develop the multiple concepts understood in the process of "toileting." Once the child has acquired the concepts, he will have the language to also communicate about his toileting needs. If a child already has this conceptual language for toileting, then a single picture (e.g., Figure 4.6) is suitable.

> ### *Activity: Why does learning concepts become a prerequisite to learning language?*

The next section presents case studies of children or youth at each of the four levels for a more detailed understanding of the concepts expressed here.

Sensori-Motor Development

Tommy

Tommy is a 4-year-old-male who responds to changes in the environment through crying, hitting, lying on the floor, screaming, and spitting. So, if he is left to do his own movements, he repeats the patterns of cups in and out, pattern puzzle pieces in and out, stacking cups and taking them apart, and so forth. In therapy for behavior, he responds to the input in the way the adult rewards him (discrete trial training[5]). Outside of therapy, however, he does not show an understanding of his actions. In other words, when a therapist or educator gives him pictures of single acts, he responds with the patterns of the act, a form of self-stimulation, but when an adult draws him into a picture or works with him by using pencil and paper, he begins to cry, scream, howl, and so on, because asking him to think rather than just respond moves him out of his comfort zone of pattern repetition.

It is necessary to move Tommy out of repeating patterns so he can learn concepts for higher functioning. Cognitively, the opportunity to think about what is in the picture or what the adult writes with him interrupts his pattern stimulation, thereby creating unknown input for him, which results in extreme negative behavior that immediately requires people to respond. People's responses to Tommy's behavior are likely to get him what he needs – the recognition of pattern repetition.

---

[5] Discrete Trial Training (DTT) is based on operant conditioning (B. F. Skinner, 1974) and is often used as a methodology to develop specific skills in children diagnosed with autism.

The brain physically uses patterns. *Only with cognitive development of concepts for language does the child developmentally grow and become independent.* For example, when Tommy begins to cry, his mother gives him different foods, changes his clothes, cools him down, gives him objects to manipulate, removes others from interrupting him, and so forth. If he eats after one of these episodes, the mother says he was hungry and that is the reason why he was crying. Mom's interpretation may or may not be accurate, however. Unless the child is able to say, "I'm going to cry and I'm not going to work until I get some cookies to eat," it is not possible to know what the child wants.

The bottom line is that this child functions in response to sensory changes. He is able to provide the same sensory types of input for adults to cognitively interpret, but he does not have enough cognitive development to express his meaning through language that is truly shared. So the constant change of patterns to what he does increases his crying tantrums because the adults' responses provide him with more new patterns.

One way to respond to a child like Tommy is to keep him compliant at specific times of the day with behavior therapy that reinforces specific patterns of response. The child sits when the teacher says, "Tommy, sit." By the teacher using specific patterns and putting the child into specific patterns of response to the teacher's patterns, the child is able to do the task. This type of pattern repetition, between what the child does in response to what the teacher does, is at the child's current sensori-motor cognitive level of functioning.

Children who are like Tommy tend to grow bigger and bigger, but their behavior outside of responding to specific patterns of therapy does not get better. To move to the next level of cognitive functioning, the child must be able to think using higher-order concepts, not just respond to sensory changes of patterns. The child's motor responses to sensory changes mean that the use of visuals must begin at the child's level and be used in a way that moves the child from a sensori-motor level to a preoperational level of cognition, one level higher than where he is currently functioning.

For Tommy, the process was slow. He was drawn into his picture doing his "work" with the teacher, Mabel. Figure 4.8 shows this first set of pictures.

Figure 4.8. **Tommy sits down to work.**

The pictures were put into a laminated folder, and Mabel and Tommy crossed the pictures off as he did his work. This provided enough new patterns so that Tommy was willing to allow Mabel (one of the authors) to H/H write with him (Mabel put her hand firmly on the back of Tommy's hand to write the patterns of what Tommy sees in the picture or what Mabel wants Tommy to be able to see in the picture). But the writing created too many new patterns that challenged Tommy's lack of cognitive development, so the kicking-screaming behaviors began again. In other words, the visuals were too complex. Tommy was not a part of the pictures.

Mabel then helped Tommy's mom draw his day so that the session with Mabel would be part of an event. The event was "Tommy's Day." As we have seen, at the sensori-motor level of cognition, the child is an extension of what he does. So, at this level, Tommy responds to the sensory input of everything in his day. His day is not made up of discrete activities. ***His being is the day that he does!*** Figure 4.8a shows a portion of Mom's drawings of Tommy's day. The whole day consisted of 37 pictures.

Figure 4.8a. **Tommy's mom draws Tommy's day.**

The cartoon of Tommy "doing his day" included working with Mabel. When Tommy came to work with Mabel (see Figure 4.8b), Mabel and Tommy would cross off the activities. In this way, Tommy could use the movement of the hand on the pictures as a way to respond to the day. Because Tommy was put into the situation as an agent to see, act, and do an activity, his work with Mabel became part of his day. Mabel then could use her cartoon of the work with Mabel to include: Tommy sees Mabel, Tommy works with Mabel, Tommy says good-bye to Mabel, and so forth.

Figure 4.8b. **Tommy and Mama after school.**

Because Tommy was able to understand the meaning of working with Mabel as part of his day, Tommy's behavior changed, and he was able to work with Mabel on more advanced concepts. And because he worked with Mabel on more advanced concepts than just learning to sit, he was able to begin to move from the sensori-motor level of thinking to the next cognitive level of development, preoperational thinking. At this level, Tommy is in his picture. He is doing the action. He is the agent.

Activity: When is it important to work on concepts with a child and then on the child's behavior?

To raise a child's thinking from one level of language development to the next, enough meaning at the child's current cognitive level must be provided. Because language concepts consist of overlapping multiple ideas, Tommy, an agent who does something, has to have multiple pictures that represent him doing multiple activities. Until Tommy could use a variety (at least three different ways of use such as his parent drawing what it looked like for Tommy to come to the clinic, what it would look like for Mabel to draw him at the clinic, and what it would look like for Mabel and his mother to draw him working at the clinic) of pictures to represent his day, he would on occasion sniffle or look like he was going to cry when he came to work. But as soon as he could see the meaning of him, as an agent, in his day of pictures, he could understand what he looked like working with Mabel.

The most important part of therapy with Mabel was for Tommy to learn to be an agent. As an agent, he no longer responded appropriately or inappropriately to patterns but was able to think of himself as an agent, someone who performed multiple acts throughout the day. He was beginning to learn concepts about himself. This learning meant that he was also beginning to think at the next level of cognition, the preoperational level.

An agent does not just respond to a sensory level of meaning. An agent responds to the actions of others or acts on objects in a way that other agents do. For example, a 2-year-old stomps her foot and says "me do it." In doing so, this child is beginning to show the development of becoming an agent. Because she is an agent, she wants to do the act by herself. Choosing to sit down instead of responding to another's stimulus "to sit down" represents a higher level of cognition. Children between 3 and 7 years of age typically use this higher, preoperational, level of thinking to act in a variety of ways on the agents, actions, and objects within their environment.

To move the cognitive level of a child like Tommy from a sensori-motor level to a preoperational level, he must be giving the opportunity to be an agent. The pictures must have maximum contrast – black-and-white drawings – and must be drawn in real time for the child to see the motor patterns of making the pictures. In other words, the pictures must depict what the child, an agent, is doing throughout the whole day.

Progress with Tommy went much faster when his whole day – home and therapy – showed him the visual meaning of his day. He had to have his pictures of where he was and where he was going with him at all times. And when he was asked to be an agent in a task, he had to cross off the pictures so he could see where he had been to begin to see himself separate from the sensory input of his world. Writing out the language meaning with the pictures for Tommy was very important. Notice that in Figure 4.8, Mom wrote the words to the pictures. In Figure 4.9, Tommy is learning about the constituents of "who," "what," and "where" so that he is learning about agents, actions, and objects. In Figure 4.9, Mabel draws for Tommy. but Mabel and Tommy write H/H. Tommy draws his first recognizable picture in the third frame.

Figure 4.9. **Tommy learns about the concepts of agents, actions, and objects.**

In Figure 4.10, Tommy is learning about content. In this case, he is learning about how he looks at the pictures of a book (agent-action-object).

Figure 4.10. **Mabel draws about the therapy task and Tommy writes H/H.**

Robin

Children who need cartoons of pictures about daily living are typically functioning at a sensori-motor level or early preoperational level. The multiples of cartoons about everything in their environment, with H/H assistance doing activities of daily living, help move them to reach a more consistent use of preoperational thinking.

Robin, a physically big 12-year-old female, was hitting. She did not have language, which means she lacked concept development. Prior to working with cartoons about all her activities of the day – and of the whole day (like Tommy) – she had received behavior and communication (speech) training for nine years and had been trained on iconic pictures.

Figure 4.11 shows the type of picture that this 12-year-old had been trained on. These pictures provided responses for some compliance, but, over time, they had not led to increased conceptualization. For example, Robin could point to the bowl for her cereal, but she could not indicate how she wanted the cereal because she did not have enough language.

***Figure 4.11.* Bowl.**

Boardmaker ™ Picture. *The Picture Communication Symbols* (PCS), Mayer-Johnson LLC (©1981-2001). Used with permission. Boardmaker™ is a trademark of Mayer-Johnson LLC.

Figure 4.12 shows an entire sequence of iconic single pictures explained with written words.

In the morning on a work day, I shower, eat my breakfast and get dressed for work. When I am ready, I sit in the chair and wait until it is time to go. Harmony drives me in the car. On Monday and Wednesday we usually go swimming first. On other work days we drive to the Carlton House first. This morning schedule is called my yellow schedule.

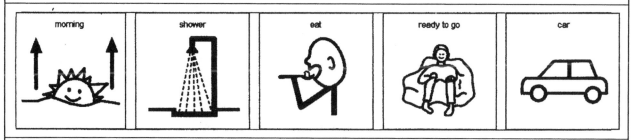

Every work day my yellow morning schedule begins with my job at the Carlton House . There I wash laundry, dry laundry, fluff clothes and hang them up on a rack so they don't get wrinkled. I work with Carol and Ellen and my job coach, Stephanie.

When my work at the Carlton House is finished I begin following my blue schedule. The blue schedule is for the afternoon. I get my lunch bag and warm up my lunch in the microwave at the break table. I will eat my lunch at the Carlton House every work day. After lunch I will get in the car with Harmony and drive to my afternoon job.

On Monday and Wednesday I work at the Little Center after lunch. I clean coolers, sort silverware and help with laundry. On Tuesday after lunch, I go to pottery. At pottery I can make anything I want to and I can paint my pieces when they are fired. Sometimes on Thursday I will mow a lawn. If it's raining I make a new plan. On Friday I go to the Chase Toddlers Center and clean the toys for the O.T.'s and other therapists.

When my afternoon job is finished I get into the car and Harmony drives me home. When I get home, both of my jobs are finished, so I can relax and choose what I want to do.

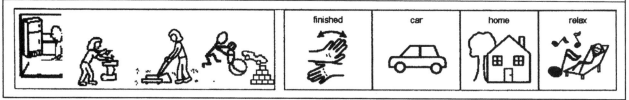

Figure 4.12. **This story was constructed by an educator using pictures from a software program called** *Picture It,* **Slater, J. (1994-2006).**
Guffey, CO: Slater Software, Inc. Used with permission.

Selecting Visuals for Behavioral Use

The written words provide the language. The pictures provide symbols that are paired with the language. For some students, this pairing of the writing with iconic or symbolic types of pictures provides sufficient language to increase conceptualization, which was the case for Robin, who is now a young adult. However, when Robin was first referred to one of the authors at 17, she was aggressive physically and did not have sufficient language to understand the iconic symbolization shown in Figure 4.12. At that time, Robin tried to use many of the various forms of communication that had been applied with her over the years, some partially intelligible speech, some sign, many cues from those who supervised her, visual schedules, and augmentative communication boards based on Boardmaker™ (Mayer-Johnson, 1981-2001). But she was not independently using these types of pictures or cuing systems, and her limited speech was difficult to understand.

The authors, along with Robin's home provider[6], began using relational types of language (Arwood & Kaulitz, 2007) with Robin, who was at that time, a young adult. Basic stick-figure types of cartooning with drawing of the concepts and H/H writing was used to help develop Robin's language so that she could understand her environment. Her aggressive behavior has decreased significantly, and she has gained enough conceptual learning so that she can use highly complex systems of communication like the one in Figure 4.12 to work at her multiple jobs. But it is important to understand that Robin, like many others, will not gain the language necessary for use of the symbolic forms of visual communication unless someone helps her develop the relational aspects (agents, actions, and objects) of language through a motor overlapping system like H/H writing along with the multiple drawn cartoons of concepts. Once sufficient language is developed, the words can be symbolized as in Figure 4.12, and these symbolizations with the writing will work in context for creating enough meaning for her to act independently. Today, anyone working with Robin always starts with drawing and writing for new ideas before moving to the symbols.

Michelle

Figures 4.13-4.15 show the work of another child (Michelle), who functions at the sensori-motor to preoperational cognitive level. Figure 4.13 shows this 6-year-old typing word patterns she has seen in her world and Mabel assigning meaning to what the child types.

Figure 4.13. **Pictures show the child the meaning of the tasks.**

The typing of random words shows that Michelle has patterns, but not the concepts of language. Mabel put these types of pattern acts into context to assign language to the acts so that the child can develop concepts, and ultimately language.

---

6   A companion home provider is a salaried person who lives with an adult providing the care that a parent would provide but without legal guardianship. In this case, Robin lived with the companion home provider in a house that had been purchased by her parents.

Figure 4.14 shows Michelle writing patterns she has learned from previous work with pictures and H/H writing from typed patterns. In this way, she is learning concepts.

Figure 4.14. **Child is learning to write patterns to drawings for concept development.**

Michelle was not talking, but she was able to learn to overlap motor patterns of typing for maintaining interaction. The adult followed the child's lead, which is characteristic of a lower sensori-motor to early preoperational child. In turn, the adult would lead with H/H writing to the adult's drawings stemming from the child's random typing of word patterns.

Figure 4.15 shows the progress that Michelle is making. She is now able to use a picture of herself thinking to make sense out of the many patterns she knows. She is learning the Language of Pictures in a way that increases her cognition and her functioning.

Figure 4.15. **Michelle and Mabel are sharing ideas about colors.**

Over a two-year period, Michelle developed enough concepts from the visual patterns to start showing a change in cognitive development. She literally moved from a sensori-motor level to a preoperational to a concrete level of understanding, even though she was not able to express her ideas at the same level.

Activity: From the cases presented, what types of visuals does a child who is at a sensori-motor level need in order to progress to the preoperational stage of cognitive development?

Preoperational Development

From the three previous case examples, it is fairly obvious that a child who continues to form patterns at the sensory level of development beyond the age of 2 experiences a severe disruption of conceptual development within his learning system. If they are severely impacted by autism, most children older than 2 demonstrate some characteristics of the preoperational level of thinking. For example, a child may sit and turn the pages of a book as if reading the book and displaying appropriate "reading" behavior, but then may begin to scream when asked to listen to someone else read the book. Turning the pages could just be patterns, but the fact that the child is looking at the book's pictures and print, in a similar fashion to readers, suggests that the child is taking meaning from the visuals on the page. If the child is able to use any academics for meaning, he is beginning to show some level of preoperational thinking. The child is thinking as he is doing something. He is an agent, who is turning the pages and looking at the visuals on the pages and then turning the pages again. His actions are in response to what he knows, not just what he senses.

It is important to understand the transition between the sensori-motor and the preoperational level of development. ***The preoperational level of thinking allows a child to make choices about what he does separate from what others do to him.*** Thus, a child at the preoperational level of cognition is able to gain tremendous knowledge about how he acts within his environment. A preoperational child is typically compliant or can be easily redirected. While such a child shows a gradual development of the understanding of everyday concepts, the world still revolves around the child at this level.

Mary

The case study of Mary provides an example of a child who exhibits a lot of pattern development at a sensory level but also some of the concepts more typical of a child who functions as an agent at the preoperational level. Mary is 9 years old. She is in an inclusionary school district where she attends third grade with the help of a paraprofessional by her side. The job of the paraprofessional is to help Mary do the class work. (Children in the sensori-motor level are not independently capable of being grouped because they do not act as agents; children in the early preoperational stage are able to be grouped but need a lot of guidance. Children at the end of the preoperational stage are easily groupable and function independently within a group without an aide.)

The paraprofessional is very good at giving the classroom work in worksheet-type activities to Mary. If the class is learning about insects, for example, Mary's paraprofessional puts the vocabulary into a worksheet, and she and Mary fill in the blanks while the rest of the class talk about the experiment they did with ants. Later Mary and the paraprofessional do another worksheet about the ants while the other students are coloring pictures to stories they wrote about their experiments with ants.

Mary's oral language is based on these worksheet patterns. For example, if the teacher asks Mary, "Tell me about ants," Mary spits back the patterns on the worksheet: "Ants are able to carry 50 times their weight." But if the teacher uses a follow-up question such as, "What would an ant carry that would be so heavy?" Mary does not understand the question. So she says, "Some ants are red and some ants are black." ***At the earliest levels of preoperational thinking, others must follow the child's thinking. The child is not maintaining a language level of conversation with another person. The adult maintains with the child. As a child develops more language for the concepts, the child finds it easier to maintain conversational topics with the adult.***

The use of worksheets to keep Mary engaged in the classroom provides sensori-motor patterns that keep Mary busy, but work on patterns does not provide the academic visuals needed to improve Mary's cognitive development. As illustrated in the case of Michelle, when the educator began to connect Michelle's patterns of typing to writing to drawn concepts, Michelle began to maintain with the adult. Michelle showed more signs of functioning in response to an adult, instead of in response to patterns. As Michelle's cognitive development increased, she showed more social as well as cognitive skills. She even began to initiate conversation. For example, she would ask her mom to call Mabel on the phone. Instead of just listening to patterns of Mabel's voice, which is what she initially did, Michelle began to use her speech synthesizer to talk to Mabel.

As Michelle's thinking became more preoperational, she initiated interactions of meaning. For example, she would point to graphic pictures on the clinic walls and ask, "What?" Then she would look at Mabel for a response and ask, "Who?" In this way she could initiate and minimally maintain a conversation. Michelle began to look like a social agent, capable of making choices about how she functioned in her world. The work on concepts with patterns moved Michelle to the preoperational level.

Mary has more language than Michelle, but the constant use of worksheets for patterns is preventing her from improving her cognitive level. Any type of pattern learning is lower than conceptual learning.

Barney

Barney is not like Michelle or Mary. Barney is an example of a child who clearly functions at the preoperational level of language. Even though he is only 6 years old, he demonstrates an understanding of the nonverbal concepts of basic semantic or meaningful relationships. For example, when he sees strangers, he asks about what they do. In therapy, he asks about the work, when he will be finished, and so on. If he does not understand a task, he asks for clarification.

Barney wants to engage with others, and he uses drawings and oral language to share what he knows about people and their relationships. These relationships reveal his recognition that he is not the only person or agent in his life but that there are also family members, teachers, and so on, in his pictures. Even though he is struggling to learn literacy skills such as reading and writing, he embraces trying different strategies that allow him to use his way of thinking. This means that he is able to see how others relate to him and how he relates to others. He is truly at the end of the preoperational level of thinking and beginning to work on the concepts of rule-governed relationships that are typical of concrete thinking (7-11 years). This suggests that even though Barney has some academic issues, he can learn at age level or higher. Barney is ready for concrete development of higher language skills (Arwood & Brown, 2001).

Activity: What are some examples of moving visually from sensori-motor to more preoperational levels of cognitive and language development?

Concrete Development

Concrete development of language refers to a shared conversation built on societal rules of how to use the conventions of language in a reciprocal way. Children and adults who work at the concrete level are able to maintain a conversation with a variety of speakers about others' interests. *A person who is functioning at the concrete level of language development understands other people's needs for communication and the social rules surrounding appropriate conversational behavior.*

With individuals who are diagnosed on the autism spectrum, social and communication behavior are usually the primary issues of concern. This means that most people diagnosed even at the high end of the spectrum lack skills in social communication (Winner, 2007a), often resulting in a preoperational form of language. This can be perplexing because the person may have lots of understanding about very formal ideas such as liberty, justice, government, osmosis, or thermodynamics, but not be able to share the conversational task very well.

Jason

Jason, who is an adolescent male, wrote the ideas in Figure 4.16. Figure 4.16 shows what appear to be very good ideas, but the language is preoperational in nature because the young man is not able to share his ideas well. The result is that the listener has to make many assumptions about what this young man writes. The adult has to interpret the meaning of what Jason wrote.

> Just thought I'd inform you a little bit on how I felt about a situation last time you came over. After I thought through what you brought up to me almost a week ago about when I walked the other way and waited on the other side when I saw you pull up until you came to the door instead of staying at the door, I kind of intermentantly escalated and compared it to the other rudes things any human being does sometimes. At times I just kind of felt deep down inside like I took it to heart and felt a little crummy about that circumstance, because of the fact that I'm a very polite gentleman, although I know it doesn't have anything to do with how many polite things I do in life ...

Figure 4.16. **A segment of a letter to Mabel.**

Assumptions in this letter include the following:

- Mabel knows what incident he is referring to.

- Mabel knows why he is writing the note.

- Mabel will read that he has feelings he wants to share.

- Mabel will know what he means by the words he uses.

This adolescent is able to think about concrete to formal ideas, but his social use of language is preoperational in nature. For example, he is not able to share the conversation with Mabel. She has to guess about what he means. To get his language to match his cognitive thinking, Jason was given many, many opportunities to connect the language patterns of writing with the iconic drawings of concepts so he could develop his own thinking.

Figure 4.17 shows an example of how Mabel drew the iconic drawing of concepts about what Jason wanted to express. This provided the pictures for his language structures.

Figure 4.17. **Mabel creates iconic drawings for the concepts of the pictures.**

However, for Jason, the drawings did not provide language, only the conceptualization. So Mabel wrote the meaning of the pictures. In this way, the Language of Pictures for Jason was in the shape of the written patterns matched to the drawn pictures, see Figure 4.18.

Figure 4.18. **Mabel provides the language of the pictures through writing.**

Jason's language is very different today. Here is a concrete level of spontaneous writing. Jason talks about the strategies he uses. Even though the language still needs some structural work, the concepts of the language are much clearer and rule-based. For example, the reader knows he is talking about his schedule and how to organize his time.

> Dear Mabel,
> Just to let you know I've been starting to fill out my schedule the way you shown me for where it says my time for appointment by adding in precise times and keeping them more in the white space and I'm mentally working my way to be more descriptive about what I need to do when I get to a specific place.

Figure 4.19. **Spontaneous concrete level of writing.**

Many people have commented on how Jason is much more fluent with conversational language. His score on an IQ test has also jumped almost two standard deviations in the two years of working on his thinking through the Language of Pictures. It is noteworthy that the only change in his life during this time was the systematic use of visuals to improve his understanding of language. Jason is now very successful at talking to others in a variety of ways, including public presentations.

Formal Development

Concrete levels of conversation are a desired outcome for most people on the spectrum, but sometimes it is very difficult to understand formal concepts. For example, taking another person's perspective is a formal social ability. Figure 4.20 shows how Aaron is taken through various developmental ways of thinking so that he can begin to understand how language goes with different levels of behavior.

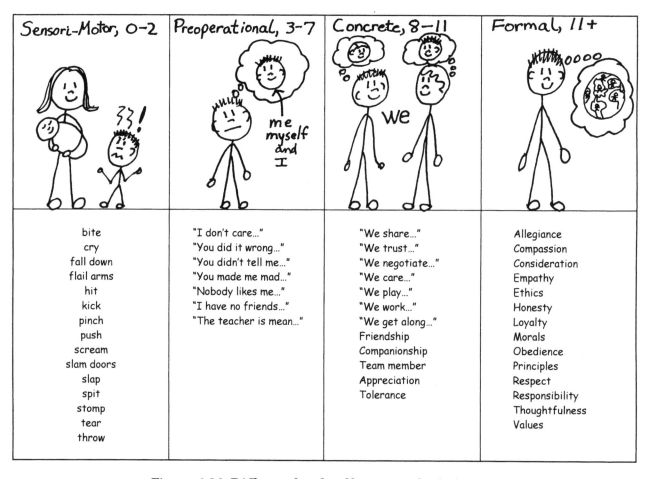

Sensori-Motor, 0-2	Preoperational, 3-7	Concrete, 8-11	Formal, 11+
bite cry fall down flail arms hit kick pinch push scream slam doors slap spit stomp tear throw	"I don't care..." "You did it wrong..." "You didn't tell me..." "You made me mad..." "Nobody likes me..." "I have no friends..." "The teacher is mean..."	"We share..." "We trust..." "We negotiate..." "We care..." "We play..." "We work..." "We get along..." Friendship Companionship Team member Appreciation Tolerance	Allegiance Compassion Consideration Empathy Ethics Honesty Loyalty Morals Obedience Principles Respect Responsibility Thoughtfulness Values

Figure 4.20. **Different levels of language for behavior.**

Aaron

Prior to Aaron learning how his behavior related to his development, he often blamed others for his actions, and he was not able to take responsibility for his actions. For example, even though he was a young adult, he had been asked to leave three different community colleges because he was disruptive in classes where he blamed the teacher and others for his lack of understanding.

Note that the pictures in Figure 4.20 represent entire stages of development and are not representative of a moving type of frame-by-frame cartoon used with a sensori-motor to preoperational child. Also note that the drawings lack the context needed for a child who responds to sensory input. This type of picture is designed to help depict the use of language expectations for rules of society, a formal way of thinking and acting from where the person is functioning.

In other words, to move a person who "should" be able to function at a formal level of behavior from the preoperational level to the concrete, preferably formal, level, the stages are drawn out showing the way the person acts at each level. The person is then confronted with two questions. In response to "Where are you functioning when you cry, scream, and yell?" most older youth and adults can look at the picture and answer, "the preoperational level." And to the question "Where do you want to function?" most will answer that they want to be at the formal level (they are older than 11). Then they work using visuals to change the behavior and language from the preoperational cognitive level to the formal, or least concrete, level.

This type of work provides a match between drawings (concepts) and writing (patterns) to create language that enables the person to think and act at a higher level. Aaron (Figure 4.20) was able to see that his behavior was often at the early sensori-motor level or preoperational level and that he had to change the way he talked and acted if he wanted to be able to function at either the concrete or formal level.

Activity: Why is it possible for a person to sometimes function at the preoperational level of cognition without knowing that he or she is at that level?

Summary

The purpose of this chapter was to demonstrate that different levels of language development necessitate different levels of pictures or visual input. The following chapters analyze in more depth the levels of the Language of Pictures to help parents and educators make better assessment and intervention decisions.

CHAPTER 5
Selecting Visuals for Behavioral Use

"Don't run" creates a picture of run.

"Don't play" creates a picture of play.

"Sit quietly" has no picture.

But "move your feet up and down" means to walk.

long the path to learning how to best use the Language of Pictures, many educators and parents find that a child's behavior often "gets in the way" of learning. So when a child tantrums, cries, or acts inappropriately, educators often focus on attempting to change the child's behavior. The adult might point, gesture, get physically big and angry in voice, or try to direct the child into compliance. ***But these nonverbal types of communications do not provide language for the child.*** Another approach is for the adult to reward the child for good behavior and try to increase the likelihood of the desired behavior occurring again through very specific sequences of reinforcement. ***But this type of focus on behavior assumes that the child's behavior is a problem.***

In fact, the child's behavior may be her only form of communication and not really a problem. That is, the child's behavior may be a symptom of what the child needs. The child may need more language or a better understanding of what the adult expects of her. For example, when a child does not respond to oral instructions or directions, rather than looking to change the child's behavior, it seems logical to try to communicate to the child the same adult expectations but in a different way.

There are many acceptable ways to communicate. However, for children with autism spectrum disorders (ASD), the communication form must be visual and the visual must be presented in context (Arwood & Kaulitz, 2007). Most important, the visual must be at the appropriate level of language and cognition for the child, as well as in a form that creates conceptual meaning for the child. For example, the adult could model the correct behavior for a child, but for many children with ASD, matching their body movements to what they see is impossible. The adult could manually sign instructions, but for some children signing is too quick and temporary. That is, once the hands finish signing, the child no longer has any visual to refer to, so the meaning is gone.

On the other hand, drawing provides a level of communication that can be seen beyond the occurrence of the behavior, and it can be adjusted to the child's language learning level. Furthermore, print patterns or writing can be used with the drawings to connect what the child looks like in a behavior and what behaviors society expects – what the child looks like is in the drawing, and what society expects is in the writing.

One of the authors has been drawing for more than 39 years to show children the meaning of behavior. It is just logical! A child who does not understand what someone says may understand what someone draws, if the level of the visual drawing matches the level of the child's thinking (see Chapter 4), the way the child learns (see Chapter 2), the child's language development (see Chapter 3), and the way the child socially sees herself. ***Behavior represents what the child knows about herself. So, behavior is a social representation of what a child thinks.*** Drawing helps assign meaning to what the child knows so that the child can learn how to behave, based on what society expects, which can be written to match the drawn pictures.

Typically, the levels of social development parallel the levels of cognitive and language development discussed in Chapter 4. The current chapter will help the reader understand why certain visuals work for behavior, a representation of our social, cognitive, and language development; and when visuals work and when they do not work to help with behavior. Finally, this chapter will bring the academic use of visuals together with the use of visuals for behavior compliance.

Social Development

A 3-year-old girl sits in front of a three-way dressing mirror smiling at her knees tucked away from her lap in the well-known "criss-cross applesauce" sitting posture. She tugs on her skirt to cover those protrusions and giggles at her hair, which flops across her face. She jumps up and lands on both feet, smiling at her new-found discovery of being able to balance on both feet at once. She then turns her head away and begins to walk, but quickly stops, as she sees someone else in the mirror.

She swings her head forward and there she is! So, where did that other person go? Who is the other person? Where is that person in the room? Cautiously, the young girl moves one hand and sees a hand move in the mirror. Then she wiggles her fingers, and sure enough, the girl in the mirror is HER!

A little bored with the mirror image "thing," she once again begins to leave her center-stage position in front of the mirror, but again catches a glimpse of someone else behind her. Quickly she turns her head back to face the mirror, peeks, and then turns her head to look over her left shoulder. There is the other girl in the mirror to her left.

"Mom, who is that?" she calls out. In response to her daughter's question, the mother comes running and sees the three images of her daughter in the three mirrors angled for dressing. Mom smiles and says, "That is you!" "No, that one, Mom" corrects the young child as she nods toward the person she sees over her shoulder in the left mirror. "That's your back side."

"What?"

"When you look into the mirror and I stand behind you, I see your front showing your face in the mirror, but I also see your back, because I am behind you. This mirror shows your front side and your back side; when you turn, you see your backside." Mom is now down touching her daughter so that the child can identify the touch with her many sides – sides that the 3-year-old is just beginning to know exist. Mom walks away as the child plays a few more minutes in front of the mirror to learn about her many facets.

For readers raised with dressing mirrors, this type of body image development is memorable. It was a magical day to learn about those sides in that mirror. It was part of normal development to see the sides the way others see them. It was a part of social development. It was the beginning of knowing what others see. It was a part of learning about how our body moves, what it looks like, and how others see our body. It was the beginning of understanding how a person, agent, relates to others visually. It was the beginning of the Language of Pictures about social development.

Activity: How is recognizing one's body in a mirror part of social development?

Many other social experiences helped develop the reader's "who." There was the day when the reader learned that the teacher did not know who she was without putting a name on the paper. Or the time that the reader discovered that fingers make shadow animals that others could see. And, there were those early experiences of reading Mom's or Dad's eyes to know what they *really mean* (Winner, 2000, 2007b).

Most people look at their parents' faces because their faces tell more of the story. For example, parents' faces are the key to whether or not one can have a special treat like a popsicle. Parents typically do not have to tell a child to look at their faces. Their faces tell their own story. And, it is not just faces that are important. The objects around the child help the child develop his sense of who he is. Remember those tables? Every time a child grows, he or she has to stand up under the table to see how tall he or she really is?! Somehow the tables keep getting shorter! But the "table process" helped the reader learn about growing and doing. What a person does results in consequences – the child stands up under a table and hits her head and learns that the table is shorter than she is.

The victories in finding identities are sweet, like the time a child learns to walk up and down the stairs without someone else's hand. Later the child wants to hold hands to show he cares. And, when the adult holds the child's hand, he gives the adult a hug – not because someone tells him "to give Grammy a hug," but because he cares that she cares. The hug represents a social connection between the two people. Children acquire their social identity in part from all of these acts that have natural consequences, such as bumping heads, as well as from what others tell children about their actions.

Activity: What role does experience play in social development?

Children develop socially from being a part of the world around them – the feel of Mom's warm arms, the softness of the couch cushions, the smell of the fresh grass while playing ball, the delight of pretend tea parties with dolls, the taste of cool popsicles. Children develop not just from the sensory experiences but also from what they see others do and from the interchanges with others – like with the dressing mirror. The concept of "who" develops from the very beginning of sensory input into that 18-month-old toddler who stomps her foot and says, "No, me do it!" By learning to do something separate from Mom's hands, that 18-month-old stomp represents a long process of growing to become a social agent with a variety of "self" components. The development of the components of "self" as an agent occurs across the cognitive and language stages.

To socially develop without intervention, children have to be able to see what others do, what they themselves do, develop language for what they see, and change their thinking about who and what they are. In "typical" development, this process unfolds smoothly and wonderfully, but for children with ASD, the patterns of what the child receives through the senses do not always create meanings that the child is able to imitate. In fact, some neuroscience (Ramachandran & Oberman. 2006; Rizzolatti, Fogassi, & Gallese, 2006) shows that for some children with ASD, the mirror neurons may not be typical. Mirror neurons are akin to what the 3-year-old child tries to explore in the mirror. She moves her hands and recognizes that those are the same hands on her body. She looks at movements in the mirror and tries to imitate what she sees.

Mirror neurons are, in part, responsible for the ability to see what others do and imitate their actions as well as be able to realize when one's own body imitates such actions. As soon as a child recognizes these types of movements, someone in the child's environment assigns meaning with language. For example, the mother says, "That is your backside." Or, "See, you raise your hand and the girl in the mirror raises her hand. That girl is you."

Some children with ASD can see another person move but are not able to automatically record how to imitate the movement. Therefore, they do not see how to move the mouth into speech or how to move the hand to draw a concept. *For most children with ASD, the whole array of social development is mysteriously shrouded in a cloak of missing language to explain who one is or to imitate what others do so as to behave the way others in the same society behave.* They don't explore their development of "self" because they don't see how their actions fit into the environment compared to what others do. They do not see how they differ from others (Grandin, 1992, 1995, 2005).

For example, children with ASD outgrow the height of a table like any other child. But a child with ASD may see that hitting one's head from standing up under the table is the result of an object hitting the child, not the result of the child outgrowing the table. A child with autism may not see himself as an agent. Because he thinks that the object, the table, caused him to hit his head, he may insist that the table be removed and another table brought into the setting. The child does not have the social language of an agent to realize that he is responsible for hitting his head. He may think the table hit him because the table is an object, not an agent. The child may even change his head position to avoid hitting the table but still not understand that he is making a choice to change head positions.

One of the authors once worked with a very tall 4-year-old child diagnosed with autism who hit his head one day under the table. For about three weeks, he would bend his knees when he walked into the room so as not to feel the pain even though he was not under the table. The child remembered that the author had helped him out from under the table by having him bend his knees. He had language to bend his knees, so that is what he did. But he did not have the language to see where his body was in relationship to his action of hitting his head, to what he did and others did to hit or not hit their heads.

Once the author drew out where he was in the room without a table over his head and where he was when he hit his head under the table and hurt his head, he looked around the room and said, "There is no table. I can walk." And then he walked without bending his knees. Every once in a while he would say, "I am not under the table. My head doesn't hurt." One day he had a headache and he said, "My head hurts; I can't stand up." He walked around with his knees bent and his head down. He needed more drawing and more language to explain how headaches occur for a lot of different reasons. So, how he gets a headache from standing up under a table was drawn along with how other headaches happen, which finally provided him enough information to have the language he needed to understand that he had not hit his head under a table.

Because this 4-year-old had enough language about his headache and about hitting or not hitting his head, he could begin to understand that his headache was not from a table. In this way, the child was beginning to gain enough mental pictures to create a vision of what it means to have a headache. The Language of Pictures for individuals with ASD is more than just using materials they can see; the Language of Pictures is about giving meaning to the child's world so that the child gains *a vision of thinking*. In this case, the child gains the information about the relationship between a table as an object and people as agents. This type of knowledge about agents and objects is learned as concepts within the first couple years of development. However, children with autism struggle with these types of concepts that others take for granted. Concepts about being an agent are social in nature. Therefore, when a child struggles to acquire the meaning of being an agent, not an object, the acquisition of this meaning affects the child's social and behavioral development.

Activity: How does language affect social and behavioral development?

A child's behavior is easily interpreted from an adult perspective. A simple response such as kicking may be interpreted as "the child does not like you." All behaviors can have language assigned to them. Without language for behavior, a child continues to physically grow and perform the same behaviors. A 2-year-old who lies down on the floor and cries when she does not have the language to ask for more juice is seen as cute and emotionally needy. Someone picks up the child and redirects the inappropriate behavior with assistance in receiving the juice. But a 14-year-old-female who functions in a general education classroom, who throws herself down and cries because she does not understand why some children need foster care, is not cute and not endearing. And, she is too big to physically redirect.

This teenager needs to see what her behaviors look like, what others think when they see her act out like this, and what the appropriate behaviors look like. Furthermore, this 14-year-old needs the drawn and written language about foster care and appropriate ways to ask questions. Without the social development of understanding the "the language of why" (why some foster care children have good homes and others do not, etc.) assigned to behavior, the child does not perceive herself as an agent, responsible for her behavior. Behavior is tied to social development from a language and cognitive perspective. The Language of Pictures for this youth is about how to make the visuals meet her learning language needs. She needs to gain a vision of thinking about who she is.

Activity: Why does behavior represent what a person knows about his own body and how others see actions of that body?

Stages of Social Development

Table 5.1 compares the neurotypical social development to the atypical social development often seen in individuals with ASD. The table shows how a combination of cognition and language by adults provides the meaning for prosocial behavior. However, without typical cognitive and language development, the child's social learning may become antisocial. Prosocial behavior increases the likelihood of a child becoming socially competent, able to initiate and maintain healthy relationships. Antisocial behavior, on the other hand, contributes to an increased likelihood of not being socially competent. One of the goals of the Language of Pictures is to provide the necessary meaning of social development for a person with diagnosed with ASD.

Table 5.1
Social Stages

Cognition	Language	Social Meaning	Typical Learning	Atypical Learning
Sensori-motor development 0-2 years	Agent-action-object language: "Me do it," "Mama juice"	Child explores the area around and begins to imitate what others do – smiles, hands on hips, reaches	Child does something, parent assigns meaning, child responds to parent – reciprocal interaction. Prosocial behavior	Child does something and parent responds; child does something different, parent acts on child. Antisocial behavior develops
Preoperational development 3-7 years old	Agent-action-object expands into structural sentences with multiple meanings of words	Child explores what she can do with others such as parallel play, independent writing and reading, invitation to play or to share	Child acts on the world around so that others assign meaning to what the child does; child changes behavior to match what others do so as to be accepted by those in the child's world; child is becoming an independent prosocial being	Child acts on those around as if they are objects, hitting or biting, for example. Adults try to suppress the antisocial behavior with punishment while trying to reward the appropriate target behaviors; child is becoming more antisocial
Concrete development 7-11 years old	Language is used to learn the rules and how to perform academics	Adults give rules about behavior in games, school, activities, home; child learns to fit into many different settings	Child is independently groupable; can sit in a classroom and engage in what others are doing that "fits" with expectations. Child explores many different activities to test out "fitting in," such as sports, hobbies, academics, etc. The child is an active prosocial, rule-governed being that fits into society	The child's antisocial behavior continues to become more aggressive without understanding the meaning behind behavior; the antisocial behavior prevents the child from fitting in. So, others must prevent violence by marginalizing, incarcerating, etc.
Formal development 11 years+	Language is the tool for academic, professional success	Society sets one standard for behavior and the individual compares societal standards to personal beliefs, values, interests; can take others' perspective or walk in others' shoes	Social competence means the individual is able not only to fit into a prosocial, democratic society but also hold personal standards for society to meet, resulting in ethical and principled behavior	The downward spiral of antisocial behavior continues, resulting in the use of medication and other ways to restrict the individual from self-inflicted harm and from inflicting harm on groups of people

Notice some important concepts about behavior in Table 5.1. First, social behavior develops in a spiral ascent of more social meaning being added. In other words, the child becomes more socially competent as meaning is added over time. For interventions to be effective, therefore, the learner must acquire meaning to change the her socio-cognitive knowledge of behavior. On the other hand, antisocial behavior spirals downward, with behavior becoming more aggressive and ultimately violent as the child gets older, or as meaning for the child continues to not develop. *A child who learns the social reasons behind her behavior is learning social concepts for social development. Utilizing the Language of Pictures, a child can begin the ascent to social competence because the visuals given at the appropriate language level provide meaning for how to fit and how to act from other people's perspectives.*

Activity: How does antisocial behavior develop compared to the way prosocial behavior develops?

In order for children to develop a more complex concept of self in relationship to others, they must have social meaning assigned to their behavior in the way they learn concepts. In this way, they learn the "why" of their behavior, which is greater than learning how to respond to others' behaviors. When children struggle with developing their social self, they often have questions. Here are some questions posed by students who are struggling to understand their social development in relationship to their behavior:

Why do I need to follow rules? How do I get a friend? How do I get a girlfriend? Why does the teacher make me sit down during reading? Why can't I hug the boys? Why do the kids laugh at the teacher's story (joke)? What is something funny? What is a feeling? Why do the boys laugh and the girls show angry faces when I use the lighter on my arm? When can I be an adult?

These questions, along with many similar ones, indicate that individuals may grow physically and even understand complex knowledge but still be functioning at a lower social level. A child who learns to imitate or respond to cues for compliant behavior is learning social skills or patterns, not concepts (Winner, 2007b).

One of the ways to positively affect the learning of social concepts is to assign meaning to behavior in the way the person learns. Since individuals with ASD learn from visual concepts that have a motor access, drawing and writing works to help develop the social concepts that behavior represents. In this way, language about behavior represents the social and cognitive development of a child. Using the Language of Pictures helps provide the necessary information for individuals with ASD to be able to choose appropriate behavior.

Activity: What are the social development stages, cognitively and linguistically?

Drawing the Meaning of Behavior

Drawing the concepts of behavior means that the visual level of the drawing must match the child's level of language learning. Figure 5.1 shows a level of cartooning for a child functioning at the sensori-motor level.

Figure 5.1. **Sensori-motor cartoon.**

From Arwood, E., & Kaulitz, C. (2007). *Learning with a visual brain in an auditory world* (p. 125). Shawnee Mission, KS: Autism Asperger Publishing Company. Used with permission.

Notice that for a child at the sensori-motor level, there must be an overlap between what the child sees and what the child does. Thinking about what the child will do is in the child's thought bubbles. This cartoon does not include writing. Figure 5.1a shows the same cartoon with writing.

Figure 5.1a. **Sensori-motor cartoon with writing.**

The writing tells the language of the pictures. For the child to acquire social concepts, the language that represents the pictures must be included with the drawings. Furthermore, unless the pictures are put with real activities into the child's real setting, the visuals will be at a higher level than the sensori-motor child can use, thus preventing the child from benefiting fully from them. For example, the cartoon in Figure 5.1 was used for a 6-year-old child diagnosed with autism. She speaks little and can be very physically antisocial, aggressively externalized through hitting, slapping, pinching, and so on.

The therapy did not begin with this level of visual but with H/H physically assigning meaning to her behavior. Table 5.2 shows the first level of therapy intervention used to help the child develop her agency so that pictures would begin to have more meaning.

Table 5.2

Sensori-Motor Level of Intervention for Language of Behavior

First seen at 4 years of age	No language; adult uses speech, gestural signs, typing, drawing of what she is doing, and H/H appropriate meaning to finger rhymes, activities with objects such as stacking cups, and ADLs	Child hits, kicks, bites, screams if adult attempts to socially connect. If left alone, child self-stims by doing same actions over and over. Adults use rewards and punishers to get her to behaviorally respond (patterns)	Intervention: Adult follows child's lead by assigning meaning to her use of stacking cups so as to begin to develop social concepts of agent-action-object; sensori-motor prerequisite to social development	Goal: to begin to develop social concept of agency: Child does something and adult assigns meaning to what child does; that is, what the child does changes what the adult does

The visuals used with the 4-year-old child were activities of daily living paired with H/H use of objects added to H/H typing on an old typewriter that allowed the child to see the strike of the letters to overlap her motor movement of her hands with the motor movement of the typing keys. In this way the child had the visual of what the hands did to produce the patterns she saw around her. Figures 5.2a and 5.2b show some of the random patterns she typed from what she saw in her environment.

```
twinkletwinkletw twwii
nle nkle
twwinkle twiinkle stacks  triangles
twinkle
stacksse dsstacksblbluesky
los
```

```
sqqare toyota
                   twinkletwinkle    stack
                                 twi,mnnn n
squarest
michelle puts circle in puzzle
```

Figures 5.2a and 5.2b. **Child types random patterns she sees in her environment.**

The person working with the child assigned meaning by signing, talking, and drawing about the activity, such as "You ride with Daddy to the clinic in his Toyota." Coupled with speech would be some manual signing (as much as the adult was capable of) along with some drawing and some other words to help explain connections. At first, the child did not follow the additional meaning, but later she began to use what she learned from this assignment of social meaning to begin to initiate acts. Table 5.3 shows the next stage of intervention.

Table 5.3

Sensori-Motor to Preoperational Assignment of Meaning for Improved Language

Child is now 5 years old	Child is beginning to say single words when there is enough overlap between motor acts (mouth, hands, strike of keys) and visual mental concepts	Child is aggressive when she does not have the meaning for her own r or others' behaviors	Intervention: Because the child is acting more as an agent – by initiating acts and by following adult actions – her ability to maintain in a social setting has improved. The adult connects the activities with drawings and writings	Goals: The child will develop the use of basic social concepts through an increase of meaning of language for agents, actions, and objects in a variety of settings

The child is beginning to move into the next cognitive level, preoperational cognition, for what she does and what others do. Still acting in the center of her world, she expects others to follow her lead. By age 7 (see Figure 5.3), the child thinks more like an agent and can see herself move through the frames of a cartoon strip. Thus, she is beginning to understand the meaning of what she does and how her behavior affects others. Only when she realizes that others are in her pictures and that their behaviors affect her and that her behavior affects others will she be able to be grouped (agents to agents) in a classroom without the use of a paraprofessional to assist her.

Notice that in Figure 5.3 the child is with another person in the picture. The presence of the additional person suggests that the child is cognitively more like a child who is 7-11 years of age. She can begin to see the relationship of herself to others. However, she is still the center of the picture, which means she functions in the preoperational level of social development.

Figure 5.3. **Preoperational level of social-cognitive development.**

The previous case of an intervention for a child between 4 and 6 years old is offered to help explain why visuals create meaning. *Visuals provide the language for behavior when used at a level that matches the child's learning system.* Using visuals includes not just the Language of Pictures that are physical but also the language of meaning of what the child sees the adult's hands do, the adult's mouth do, the adult's body do, and so on. In order for a child to develop the social meaning of behavior, the adults must assign meaning in ways that make sense to the child's learning system. For children with ASD, the meaning must be visual. But without the motor patterns of the mouth or the motor patterns of the writing movements of the hand, they may not be able to acquire the language concepts of the social meanings of what they see. The motor movements create the visual shapes of the concepts of what a child with ASD recognizes.

Activity: What are some ways that a person could assign meaning with the motor component of visuals?

Different Types of Visuals for Behavior

Since behavior represents the child's social and cognitive ability to perceive how he acts in relationship to the expectations of others, it is not until the child has a concrete level of language that he can act the way a group of people expect. Visuals such as drawings, cartoons, and so on, are used to help the child learn to put him into a picture, so he can act the way he perceives the picture.

Figure 5.4 shows how Niki, a child similar to Michelle in the previous section, begins to assign meaning to her own typed patterns. At this point, the child expects the other person in the picture to respond. This means that cognitively and socially the child is developing more language through pictures and for pictures. Figure 5.4 shows how Niki is beginning to show conceptual meaning for her random typed word patterns.

| Later, Niki types "tangrams" and points to the box on the floor. | Teacher says, "I don't see any tangrams ... I don't know what you mean." | Niki then types, "tangrams plus." | Teacher says, "Tangrams are pictures that are made from shapes." |

Figure 5.4. Child shows a preoperational understanding of concepts about two people.

From Arwood, E., & Kaulitz, C. (2007). *Learning in a visual world with an auditory brain* (p. 272). Shawnee Mission, KS: Autism Asperger Publishing Company. Reprinted with permission.

For a child's social understanding to be refined, her Language of Pictures must increase. Figure 5.5 shows how the cartoon with writing increases the meaning of the child's behavior by adding more cartoons or layers to her understanding.

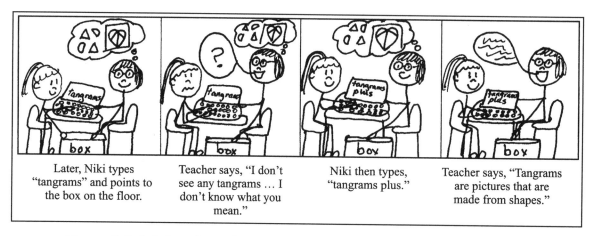

| Later, Niki types "tangrams" and points to the box on the floor. | Teacher says, "I don't see any tangrams … I don't know what you mean." | Niki then types, "tangrams plus." | Teacher says, "Tangrams are pictures that are made from shapes." |

Figure 5.5. Adult refines the meaning of the child's concepts by adding more pictures and thus more language.

From Arwood, E., & Kaulitz, C. (2007). *Learning in a visual world with an auditory brain* (p. 272). Shawnee Mission, KS: Autism Asperger Publishing Company. Reprinted with permission.

The child continues to communicate, and the adult continues to refine the meaning of what the child types. In this way, the adult provides more meaning for the child to increase her social and cognitive development through the increase of the Language of Pictures. Remember, the writing forms shapes, which are also pictures, not words, for children with ASD who function at this language level. See Figure 5.6.

| Again, Niki types "tangrams plus" and points to the box. | Teacher says, "I like to play with tangrams. Niki, do you like to play with tangrams?" | Niki types, "play with tangrams." | Teacher takes the tangrams out of the box for Niki to use. |

Figure 5.6. Adult continues to assign meaning.

From Arwood, E., & Kaulitz, C. (2007). *Learning in a visual world with an auditory brain* (p. 272). Shawnee Mission, KS: Autism Asperger Publishing Company. Reprinted with permission.

Figures 5.7 and 5.8 are excellent examples of how the teacher continues to assign a refinement of meaning, while giving the child the necessary language to request objects and actions and, therefore, be socially appropriate. By developing the language about the social appropriateness of making a request, the child is learning concepts, not just patterns, and therefore is growing both cognitively and linguistically. Because learning is a socio-cognitive process, the child is also learning how to be an agent and is, therefore, developing social concepts.

Figures 5.7 & 5.8. Assigning more language.

From Arwood, E., & Kaulitz, C. (2007). *Learning in a visual world with an auditory brain* (p. 273). Shawnee Mission, KS: Autism Asperger Publishing Company. Reprinted with permission.

Notice that in the previous figures, the child is working on both academic and social concepts. By acquiring a foundation for how to do academic work in an appropriately social way, the child is learning prosocial behavior. Prosocial learning takes the place of antisocial development. Since conceptual learning is both social and cognitive in nature, the child is learning concepts that help her behave in a prosocial way while also learning about the concepts of the activities. Because this child, like many children with ASD, sees little meaning in the picture at this level of language, movement of the hands, mouth, and body to create shapes of spoken or written word patterns along with signs and gestures provide the child with visual mental shapes of the motor movements. In other words, the motor movements provide the child with the Language of Pictures.

Activity: How do motor tasks like typing and H/H writing provide patterns to match the pictures (concepts) to create language?

Learning to Behave in a Prosocial Way

There are two major ways to look at the use of visuals for behavior:

1. If the child can see what she does in the visual, she is more likely able to match her behavior to the picture.

2. If the child has limited meaning about how to behave, the visual provides the language needed for her to act in a prosocial way.

Whether the child uses the visual to match how she looks or to begin to develop more meaning or language about how to choose to behave, visuals can be used to assign more meaning to a child's behavior. All children learn to behave. Whether a child has the choice to behave a certain way or not depends on whether he has the language to choose to behave a particular way. ***Children who are diagnosed with ASD learn to behave in the way their learning systems turn patterns into new concepts. In other words, they learn to behave by acquiring the meaning of social behavior through motor acts that create mental shapes of visual concepts.***

Activity: How do children with ASD learn to behave in a prosocial way?

Because children with ASD need to acquire the visual shapes of ideas through motor patterns, simply using any set of visuals does not cause the Language of Pictures to result in prosocial behavior. In other words, just showing a child with ASD a picture of how to look when he is supposed to do something does not provide him the language of the picture being shown. Also, modeling the behavior depicted in the picture may not provide the Language of the Pictures. Further, offering a reward paired with a child's prosocial behavior as a way to reinforce or increase the likelihood of the child to perform the behavior again may create an association between the reward and task, but it may not provide the Language of the Pictures for the child. Instead, the child with ASD may need to see the visual patterns of meaning such as with print or type or mouth movements to which pictures are added for the language to be developed.

Chapter 4 introduced Tommy, a child whose behavior was "out of control." Mabel drew the pictures before Tommy came so that he could see himself in the expected tasks. But at the time he did not have the language for the pictures, even with H/H drawing and writing. Figure 5.9 shows the first schedule.

Figure 5.9. **Tommy's first schedule for therapy.**

Since Tommy did not have the language for the print and pictures, he had trouble meeting behavioral expectations. As soon as Mabel started to work with him, she realized that Tommy needed more layers of motor patterns to form visual concepts. So she redrew the schedule. Figure 5.10 shows the second schedule with the many layers of motor movements necessary to turn the motor patterns into concepts. When Tommy received the information through his motor movements, he was able to behave appropriately and follow the session activities. Note that Tommy needed about 12 different layers of motor patterns to create the necessary visual-motor patters to form shapes to create visual concepts.

Figure 5.10. Tommy's second schedule with more language attached to the pictures.

The layers of information that Tommy needs are all the different ways that Mabel inputs the meaning or language, as well as the different ways she assigns meaning so that Tommy can do the task. By providing him several different ways to say, sign, write, draw, rewrite, draw, sign, and so on, Tommy was able to create more shapes of motor patterns so he can learn the language concepts.

Activity: Why did Tommy need more language, instead of less language?

Just like neurotypical learners acquire the meaning of behavior through the use of the spoken language to tell them what to do and how to do what they are supposed to do, *children with ASD can learn to behave by acquiring the mental visual concepts of what they see move.* Many children with ASD do not attend to the drawings because the pictures have little meaning. However, most children with ASD will attend to someone writing and can often represent exactly what they have seen written even without knowing letters or the names of the ideas they are able to write.

Visual Thinking Strategies

This ability to understand the meaning of the print comes from the shapes of the printed letters.
That is, the shape of the hand writing an idea is as important as the shape of a picture of an idea. Movements of the mouth and hands make shapes. Figure 5.11 shows some work with Tommy where only the shapes of ideas (configurations) are used to help attach language to the meaning of the concept "swim."

Figure 5.11. **Tommy begins to understand the concept "swim."**

Activity: Why do shapes provide the language of concepts?

Shapes of ideas are like puzzle pieces. Most children with ASD are fascinated by the visual patterns that they can create with movement. So they twirl, flip, bonk, or flap, creating motor patterns over and over. By turning letter shapes into the concepts of language by matching patterns of ideas in context with the picture and meaning in print, children with ASD learn to write, then read, and speak. All of this learning contributes to more appropriate behavior. Figure 5.12 shows a child beginning to see the patterns of concepts in shape form.

Figure 5.12. **Child learns the shapes of patterns to form concepts.**

From Arwood, E., & Kaulitz, C. (2007). *Learning in a visual world with an auditory brain* (p. 139). Shawnee Mission, KS: Autism Asperger Publishing Company. Reprinted with permission.

Remember from Chapter 4 that the meaning of a picture depends on the level of language the child brings to the picture? For example, the child may not recognize the head of a lion as a lion without the context of the lion's body, the grasslands where it lives, and so on. The shapes of ideas of print are the same. The child may not recognize the meaning of a shape without the context. Figure 5.13 shows a complete sentence that has been bubbled.

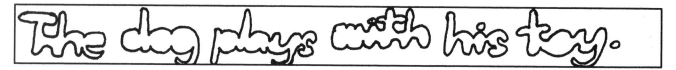

Figure 5.13. **Bubbling an entire sentence.**

From Arwood, E., & Kaulitz, C. (2007). *Learning in a visual world with an auditory brain* (p. 254).
Shawnee Mission, KS: Autism Asperger Publishing Company. Reprinted with permission.

A child who needs to see the pattern of the shape as part of a story must be able to see how shapes form meaning. This meaning comes from the similarities and differences of shape. In this way, the child is able to perceive the language of the shapes as pictures with unique meanings. Without the contrast of the way the letters create shapes, a child may not be able to recognize the meaning. Figure 5.14 shows the frame of two words but without the shapes of the ideas. In this way, the word is highlighted, but the meaning is not distinct.

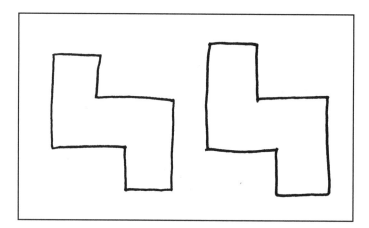

Figure 5.14. **These are the frames for the words "dog" and "log."**

When the shapes are in contrast to one another and show the image of an idea that is distinct, the child sees a puzzle of pieces that make meaning. Figure 5.15 shows the same framed words as bubbles, with distinct meaning or shapes.

Figure 5.15. **Bubbling "dog" and "log."**

The shapes of ideas (words), along with the movement of the hand to create shapes attached to pictures or concepts, creates the Pictures of Language for individuals with ASD. Children with ASD can learn how to behave by acquiring not only the mental concepts of what they look like and do, but also the language of what the concepts or pictures mean.

Activity: How does bubbling patterns even when children can't read, along with drawings, create the language for behavior and other academic abilities like reading, writing, and speaking?

Summary

Visuals can be used to help a child with ASD learn to see the appropriate behavior, especially when the visual is paired with print, as print assigns meaning to the visual through language. Language may also be provided by speaking, but most children with ASD learn concepts best by seeing the shape of movements to create a vision of thinking. The Language of Pictures for children with ASD may include gestures, sign language and, most important, print.

For a child with ASD, learning to behave in a prosocial way is being able to learn the language of what she sees. A child can only see what she has language for and can only learn to behave if the meaning of her actions is given language. Print in the form of shapes provides the language of the pictures for many children with ASD, which results in a vision of thinking.

CHAPTER 6
Selecting Visuals for Social Use

I can connect the strings

but not the people.

I see strings

but not the faces.

Kathy sat in a sixth-grade desk, skirt overflowing the bottom rungs, legs apart, and feet wrapped around the front legs of the desk. She smiled while the teacher chastised the classroom of students for their unacceptable behavior on the playground during morning recess. Kathy's arms stretched out across the desk, and with fingers curled over the front of the desk, she raised a single finger at a time and gently flipped the long brown hair of the girl sitting in front of her.

The middle-aged woman sitting next to her said, "Kathy, no. Don't touch her hair." Kathy began to giggle as the teacher at the front of the room continued to scold the students for being disrespectful to the recess duty teacher. Kathy had intentionally been seated at the back of the room so that her assistant, Mrs. Boggs, could quietly work with her. Mrs. Boggs, the lady sitting next to Kathy, immediately explained, "This is not funny. Don't laugh." But for Kathy, how could this not be funny? The teacher's frown formed deep lines like strings across a table, the kind of strings used to play a favorite pattern game of "Cat's Cradle." Kathy loved to play that game!

Kathy suddenly stood up and raised the bottom of her skirt up over her head to rearrange her slip, causing Mrs. Boggs to immediately to pull Kathy down into her chair. The teacher looked at Mrs. Boggs, who then raised Kathy's elbow as a physical cue to help Kathy walk out of the classroom. Kathy had disrupted the flow of the classroom. Kathy's behavior was "antisocial" because it did not promote the well-being of prosocial or acceptable classroom behavior as defined by the teacher and the school.

The development of appropriate prosocial behavior is the result of learning the meaning of what a person sees, touches, hears, tastes, and smells. The meaning for these sensory experiences forms concepts that prosocial members of society put into language. These members subsequently use that language to describe the behavior. For example, seeing another person's feet go up and down is called "walking" by societal members. The previous chapter explained how visuals help assign meaning to behavior. This chapter describes the journey to prosocial learning through the use of the Language of Pictures.

Social Development of Meaning

Kathy, a sixth-grade student, diagnosed with autism and capable of doing grade-level academic work, is assisted by a paraprofessional, Mrs. Boggs, all day, every day. Kathy has the academic ability of grade-level students but not the social development.

Social development consists of stages that reflect the cognitive use of meaning as well as the language development of meaning (see Chapter 2). For example, a child at 3-5 years of age is able to watch others' behaviors; and, with the language of a prosocial adult, this child is able to work in small groups of children without the constant assistance of an adult (see Tables 5.2 and 5.3). Between 5 and 7 years of age, a child is able to use enough personal language to assign meaning to what others do to understand the rules for working with others in groups without adult help. By 8 years of age, a child is able to understand the rules for being grouped into classrooms of 30-40 or more students (such as in P.E., extracurricular activities like orchestra, attending church, etc.) without needing the constant help of an adult.

For Kathy and others with an autism spectrum disorder (ASD), it is important to realize that the ability to function independently is a direct result of good use of functional language for prosocial behavior. Prosocial behavior consists of acts that are acceptable by society for the purpose of furthering the development of others in society. To be prosocial, a person with ASD needs to have the language of the pictures of what it looks like to be prosocial.

Because prosocial behavior requires an understanding of how our behavior promotes the well-being of others, to become prosocial means that we must be able to *see* other people in our mental pictures. For example, a teenager diagnosed with high-functioning autism insisted that he was going to sing at a concert. His language sounded like this, "I will sing at the concert Friday night." The listener asked, "What time is the concert?" He responded, "I don't know. I sing Friday night." "Who is the concert for?" "I think it is for school." "Is the concert at the high school?" "YES, the choral group." "Are you in the choral group?" "No, I sing at school." "So, if the concert is at the high school, is the high school choral group singing?" "I don't know."

As the reader might begin to realize, the person who is talking about singing is not able to relate his own mental thoughts about what he does to others so as to explain the process of who is singing, where he is singing, when he is singing, and so on. After telling many people about his recital, this young man was disappointed when people he had told about his singing did not show up to hear him sing. He did not realize that his inability to communicate adequately – how to appropriately ask others to attend his singing recital – was a problem with language development representative of his social understanding. He had plenty of language structures and vocabulary to tell others about his activities. However, he lacked the language of his social development, indicating that he did not understand how others perceive the meaning of his words or the lack of words. He did not see how his behavior affected others' behaviors. He did not have the Language of Pictures for what he needed to tell people so that they could plan to attend his recital. To develop the language for his social development, he needed someone to write the rules about how to communicate to others so as to develop prosocial behavior.

Figure 6.1 is about the prosocial rules of being a friend. Anna is learning about the language of the pictures she needs to understand being a "friend." The writing provides the language patterns that go with the drawn concepts that connect with the prosocial behaviors related to the language. In this way, Anna is learning not only a concept as a definition but the behavior related to the concept. Writing forms a picture of patterns that provides the language for the concepts.

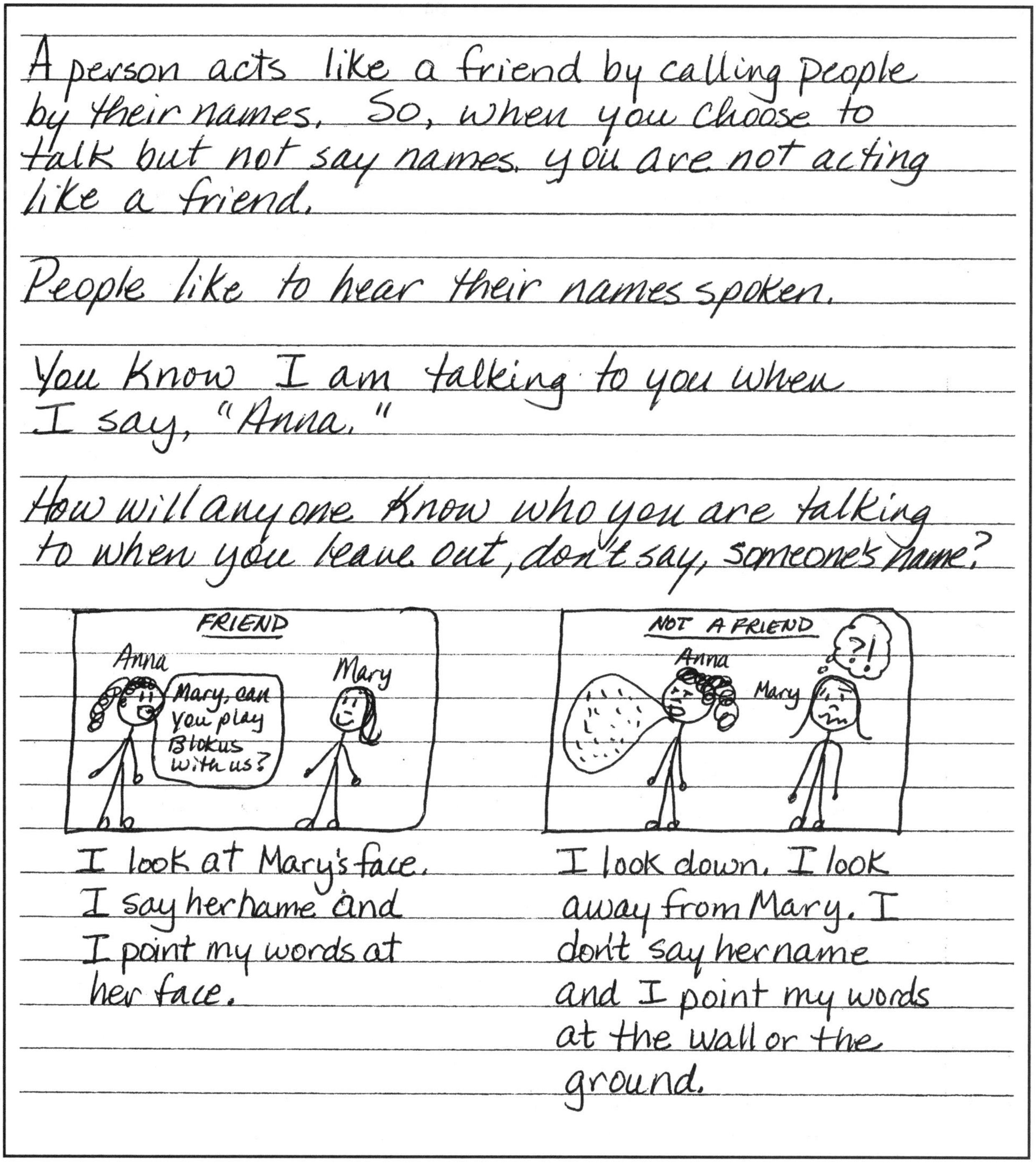

A person acts like a friend by calling people by their names. So, when you choose to talk but not say names, you are not acting like a friend.

People like to hear their names spoken.

You know I am talking to you when I say, "Anna."

How will anyone know who you are talking to when you leave out, don't say, someone's name?

FRIEND

Anna
Mary, can you play Blokus with us?
Mary

NOT A FRIEND

Anna
Mary

I look at Mary's face. I say her name and I point my words at her face.

I look down. I look away from Mary. I don't say her name and I point my words at the wall or the ground.

Figure 6.1. **Anna is learning about talking to another person.**

As part of being a friend, Anna wanted others to engage in various activities with her such as playing a game, but she did not know what to say or how to invite a person to join her. Anna could produce the sentences as skills and she could tell the rules of an invitation, but she was not developing the concepts about "inviting others." Therefore, she was not acting in prosocial ways when she wanted to invite others to play games, and so on.

In Figure 6.2, Anna learns about "agency" or "who" she will invite as part of the speech act of "inviting" someone.

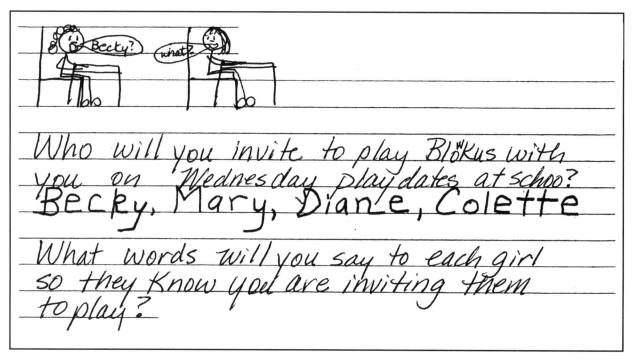

Figure 6.2. **Anna is learning how to invite others to play a game.**

To invite someone is a language act. Some language acts perform specific functions and are called *performatives*. To invite a person is a type of performative. A performative language act is one that results in affecting a social relationship between two or more people because of the language shared in the behavior or act. These types of language functions are important in the development of prosocial behavior. Figure 6.3 shows the type of language used to match Anna's intentions.

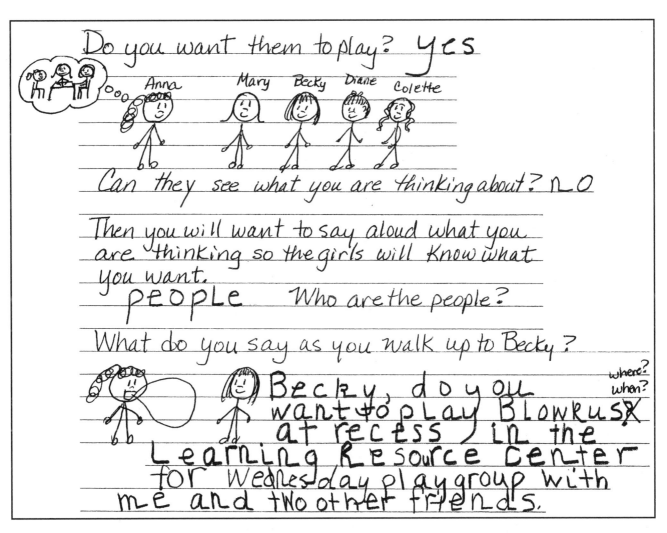

Figure 6.3. Anna learns about what she is thinking and what others are thinking about when inviting others to play a game.

Activity: What is a performative?

Other performatives include concepts such as marry, vow, promise, lie, steal, collaborate, swear, and request. All of these concepts create a social relationship where two or more people understand both parties' roles in the language act. For example, with the performative of marry, two people engage in the mutual decision to create a publicly recognized relationship. Both parties expect the other person to understand what the word "marry" means to each. In reality, this does not always happen, but then the marriage does not work as a performative and the act of "marriage" is dissolved – another performative occurs.

The absence of Anna stating that she wants others to play with her is also a type of performative. This type of absence of oral language indicates a lack of personal desire to be with others. Figure 6.4 shows Anna creating a different picture through her words than she does with a note. Anna is learning how language creates pictures of intentional prosocial behavior between people that objects like notes do not.

Figure 6.4. **Anna wants others to have a relationship with her.**

Activity: Why is a note impersonal? Hint: What is the difference between an object or a "what" and a person or an agent ("who")?

These performatives are language functions. Language functions are the processes of how language works to develop social and cognitive development. There are a couple of ways to think about social development. One way is to think about teaching behaviors that others interpret as socially appropriate skills. For example, a child is taught to shake hands and introduce himself to others. These are "social skills."

The second way of thinking about social development is to consider the social concepts underlying the skills. For example, being able to "introduce" oneself is a type of performative. Introductions have numerous semantic rules. When do you introduce yourself? Do you always introduce yourself the same way? Who wants an introduction? Why would I introduce myself if the person already knows me? But a basic understanding of the concepts underlying the ability to "introduce" oneself requires a social understanding of others and of others' concerns. This understanding of others' needs is greater than the individual development of social skills such as shaking hands and saying one's name.

Figure 6.5 shows how Anna struggles to understand that she cannot control what others think, only how she acts. In this way, a performative is greater than the parts of a language act. The parts of skills may be used inappropriately without understanding the meaning of the underling concepts. Being able to understand how others think, and therefore thinking about others, raises Anna's cognitive understanding of social development as well as her behavior.

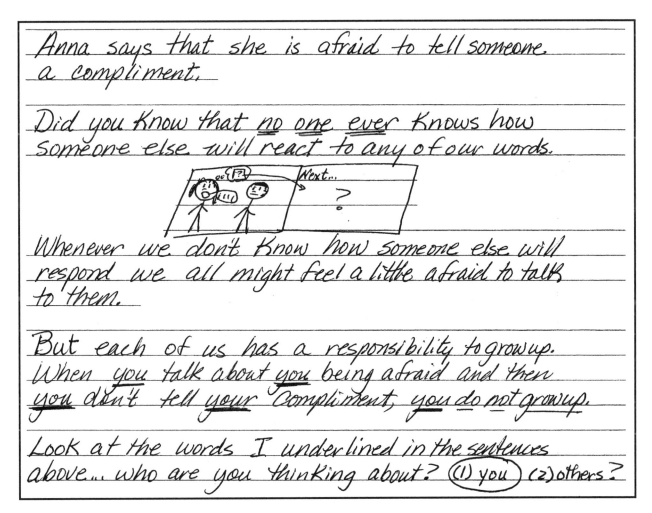

Anna says that she is afraid to tell someone a compliment.

Did you know that no one ever knows how someone else will react to any of our words.

Whenever we don't know how someone else will respond we all might feel a little afraid to talk to them.

But each of us has a responsibility to growup. When you talk about you being afraid and then you don't tell your compliment, you do not growup.

Look at the words I underlined in the sentences above... who are you thinking about? (1) you (2) others?

Figure 6.5. **Anna learns that she does not control what others think and that worrying about her impression is not thinking about others' needs.**

Activity: Why does a language act that represents two or more people in a relationship provide meaning for developing prosocial behavior?

Single pictures of what a person does in developing social skills such as shaking hands and saying one's name help develop social skills. However, to understand social concepts that require an understanding of multiple relationships between the speaker and others around the speaker. Therefore, multiple visuals or pictures must be used with language.

The written and oral language explains the meaning of the concepts of the drawn pictures. When Anna worries about what she needs, what she says, what she does, and what she thinks, she is functioning at a preoperational level. That is, conceptually, her social development is that of a child between 3 and 7 years of age. She is not thinking about how her acts affect others and how others feel because of her acts. If she were thinking about others, her behavior would be more like that of a child between 7 and 11 years of age. Figure 6.6. shows Anna's social development in relationship to her chronological age.

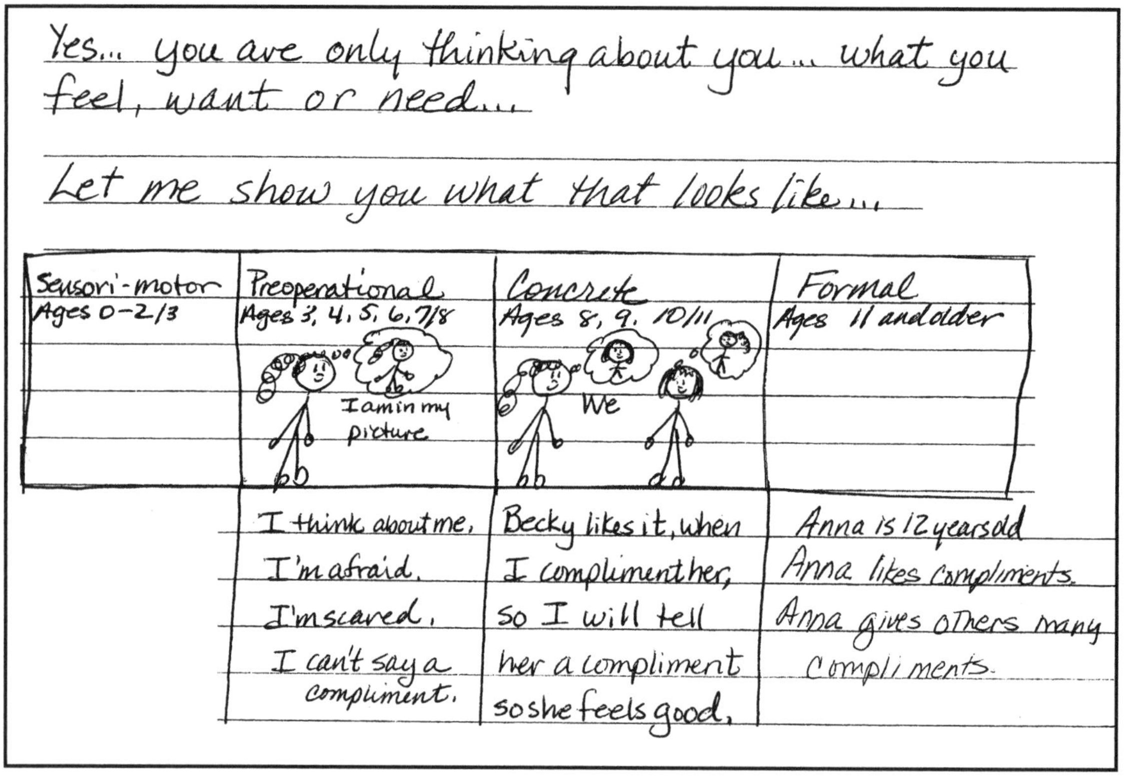

Yes... you are only thinking about you... what you feel, want or need...

Let me show you what that looks like...

Sensori-motor Ages 0-2/3	Preoperational Ages 3, 4, 5, 6, 7/8	Concrete Ages 8, 9, 10/11	Formal Ages 11 and older
	I am in my picture	We	
	I think about me, I'm afraid. I'm scared. I can't say a compliment.	Becky likes it, when I compliment her, so I will tell her a compliment so she feels good,	Anna is 12 years old Anna likes compliments. Anna gives others many compliments.

Figure 6.6. **Anna learns that her language behavior is more like that of a young child.**

Activity: How is Anna learning that her language paints a picture of her behavior?

For some students, the purpose of social lessons is to teach social skills. Therefore, these types of single pictures that emphasize social skills, such as a single picture of a child shaking hands with another child, will work. However, *social competence is the ability to initiate and maintain healthy relationships, which means that it is important to conceptually understand how one's behavior affects another person.* Social responsibility requires more than skills; it requires an understanding of a person's behavior in relationship to others. Figure 6.7 is a written explanation to help Anna understand that she is solely responsible for her behavior and that others are responsible for their behavior.

We can't control other people. We can only control ourselves. When other people choose to act badly or to behave in unexpected ways, their 'bad' or unexpected behavior reflects who they are. Their bad or unexpected behavior has nothing to do with you.

Figure 6.7. **This is the written explanation for Anna's behavior and that of others.**

Anna struggles with understanding how her behavior is or is not like someone else's behavior. She does not understand that to be socially responsible for her behavior, she must think about the needs of others. Figure 6.8 is a cartoon with writing used to help Anna understand some of these conceptual relationships.

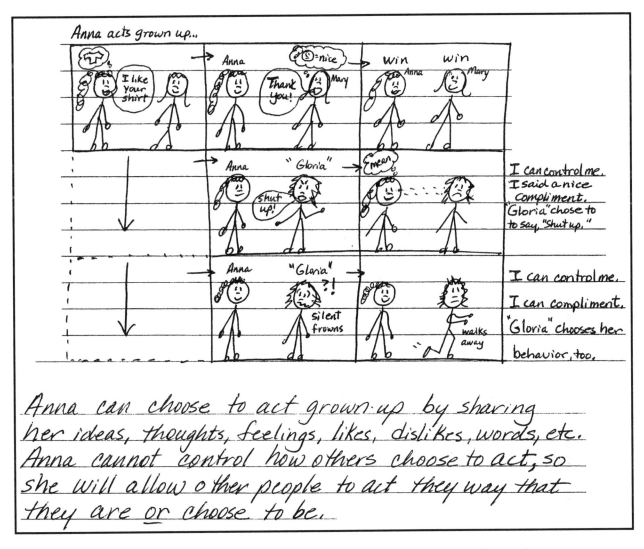

Figure 6.8. Anna learns how to understand others' acts in relationship to her own acts.

Prosocial development is based on developing healthy relationships. Figure 6.8 shows the written explanation of why Anna may choose to be around people who show predictable behavior. Anna is learning that others are responsible for their behavior just as Anna is responsible for her behavior. Others choose to be around those who show predictable behavior. For example, when Anna's behavior is predictable, others want to be around her (see Figure 6.9).

> I prefer to be around people who act in more expected ways. People who act in expected ways make good friends. People who behave badly or act in unexpected ways do not make good friends.
>
> As you grow up you will benefit from choosing people who act in expected ways to be your friends.

Figure 6.9. Anna learns why she wants to use predictable or expected behavior.

Anna sometimes has meltdowns when she cannot understand others' behavior. Yet, when others have meltdowns, she does not understand how to comfort them. Being a friend, performing acts like meeting, greeting, or inviting, and learning to be prosocial with others requires multiple sets of pictures and multiple examples of prosocial meaning. Anna also wants to act with others through email, notes, and other impersonal methods that are not prosocial.

Figure 6.10 shows how Anna is learning to do for others what she would like others do for her. In this way, she is learning the Language of Pictures for social concepts about who she is in relationship to others. The ability to be more concrete or rule-governed in her understanding necessitates the use of lots of visuals (for example, Figures 6.1-6.11) that connect what she sees (pictures or drawings) necessary with the language (print or written form) to develop the higher social concepts.

Figure 6.10. Anna learns about how others treat her.

The story of the Language of Pictures is complex for social concepts. For example, Anna must learn that she does for others what she wants others to do for her. In Figure 6.11, Anna learns that what she feels from getting something from others is how others feel from what she provides them. In other words, there is a reciprocal relationship.

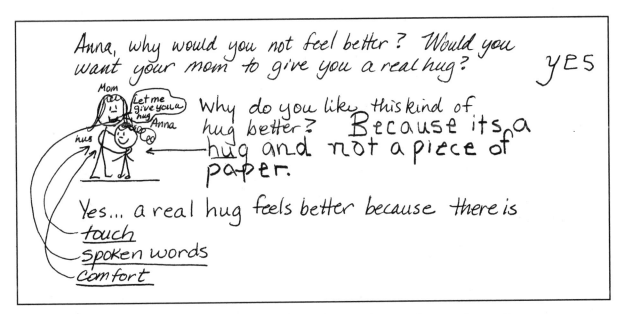

Figure 6.11. **Anna learns about how a hug is better than a piece of paper.**

Social as well as cognitive development necessitates an understanding of the underlying reciprocity between a person and others. Learning and understanding concepts like being a friend requires that a person learns to provide what others need through language functions. Thus, language functions help develop prosocial behavior. Language functions for social development represent cognitive concepts such as respect, consideration, empathy, friendship, collegiality, nurturance, justice, self-esteem, self-concept, acceptance, reciprocity, emotion, tolerance, open-mindedness, and so forth. These types of formal social concepts require a "story" of visuals to explain not only the meaning of the words but (a) the underlying concepts about relationships among people, their actions, and their objects; (b) the rules among these people, their actions, and their objects; as well as (c) the multiple ways that these concepts develop through performatives and other types of language functions.

The person with an ASD needs to *see* the oral language as a written pattern connected to multiple pictures to develop formal social concepts since writing in real time creates the shapes of words as visual mental pictures needed to acquire the higher-order concepts. Figure 6.12 takes Anna back to how to talk or invite her "friends" to a playgroup so that they will want to come.

Figure 6.12. **Anna learns how her words and her behavior relate to how others understand her intent.**

For Anna, at least 12 different sets of relationships have been written about, talked about and, in some cases, drawn to create the Language of Pictures about the language function of "invite." All formal concepts such as performatives like "invite" or concepts like "respect" or "responsibility" require a complete story of the relationships that make up the concepts.

Activity: Why is it important to connect all the individual rules about how to invite someone?

Social Determination

Social determination is a concept that refers to what we need to know in order to act like others in our dominant culture. The culture determines what we need to do to act socially appropriately. Society develops the Language of Pictures for what is appropriate and not appropriate. For a child, how adults assign meaning to his behavior determines the rules the child begins to learn about his social development. For example, if a child fusses by hitting and kicking and the parent explains his behavior by saying he is tired, the child will learn that "fussing" is the way to get time to take a nap. Even after the behaviors of hitting and kicking are replaced with more appropriate behaviors such as whining or crying, the child will still "fuss" when he is tired. Even into adulthood, this person will "need" to take a nap and others will excuse the antisocial behavior with something like "he gets so cranky if he doesn't get a nap."

Determining social development is a process of assigning prosocial meaning to a child's earliest behaviors. Providing the meaning of prosocial behavior for individuals with ASD requires the use of visuals that meet their cognitive and social development for language. Social determination is a gift that parents and teachers provide a child when they provide prosocial meaning to his behavior. Giving prosocial meaning requires an emphasis on social development, not social skills. For individuals with ASD, prosocial meaning comes from the use of visuals that provide the social meaning of the Language of Pictures.

Activity: How do others help determine social behavior?

So when does a child need just social skills? Concepts always underlie the natural development of skills. When a child is developing in a typical way, behaviors represent what she understands socially. A tantrum means the child does not understand that her acts or behaviors affect others. Without this understanding, the child does not develop the necessary skills to prosocially communicate her needs. As she develops an understanding that a tantrum does not provide her with the results she expects, she changes her behavior to better meet her needs. In this way, behavior changes as the child understands more of what is conceptually understood by those in the child's environment. Thus, her skills improve as her underlying social concepts develop.

The behaviors of children with ASD also show what they socially understand. For example, a tantrum means the child does not have the cognitive development to recognize his needs, the language development to express those needs, as well as the social development to use behaviors that are more likely to work for the betterment of others. To be able to demonstrate the prosocial behavior that has been determined by the dominant culture, socially, a child with ASD needs the same social development underlying social skills as a neurotypical child.

Activity: How do concepts underlie typically developing social skills?

Behavior that contributes to the well-being of others is prosocial behavior. Behavior that contributes to the detriment of others is antisocial behavior. Both types of behavior can get one's basic needs met.

For example, antisocial behaviors such as seen in a tantrum might get others to move the child into a dark, quiet spot to help the child calm down. Thus, the child tantrums to get away from a particular input, to be removed from others' acts, to be alone, and so on. But these types of behaviors are not prosocial. The tantrum results in the child being removed from what she might actually want. For example, if the child tantrums to get a snack; but, in response to the tantrum, the adult removes the child from the eating area, then the tantrum did not get the child what she needed, a snack. In this way, the tantrum is antisocial. Removing the child from the eating area because the child tantrums does not provide the child with what the child needs to do to get a snack when she is hungry. By removing the child from the eating area, the adult is contributing to the child's antisocial behavior. The child has one intention underlying her behavior, to obtain a snack; and the adult interprets the child's behavior in a different way. Without the language for how to request the snack in an appropriate way, the child continues to grow bigger and more antisocial in her behavior. As a result, at 12 years of age, she might still be tantruming.

To become prosocial, the child needs the language that represents the prosocial meaning of the concept of asking for food when she is hungry. Removing the child to a dark place to calm down does not give the child the concepts of what she could do to be prosocial. To become prosocial, the child must develop the concepts about how to ask for a snack or obtain a snack when she is hungry so that she is effective in receiving the snack and so the adults are able to maintain a social interaction. (When she is removed to calm down, there is no social maintenance between the adult and the child.) By developing the language of the concepts, the child begins to understand the meaning of actions. In this way, she is able to make a prosocial request such as "I am hungry, so I was wondering when it will be snack time." The child realizes (a) that other people are not eating; (b) that he is hungry, but that this is not the time to eat; and (c) that he is also able to problem solve regarding his needs.

Figure 6.13 is an example of a cartoon used with a student who complained about what others did to him. The result of his verbal tantrum with the teacher was that he still had to use the bathroom but did not want to go. The "pull-down" options of using different cartoons shows different choices of behavior based on different meanings that go with the different sets of pictures.

Figure 6.13. **The child can choose which set of behaviors he wants to use if he has the language for those behaviors.**

The teacher used a lot of words with the drawing of the cartoon choices in Figure 6.13. For some children, more writing than drawing is needed.

For a different child, Owen, the teacher wrote out the information that he needed to learn from. Figure 6.14 describes the situation leading to the drawing of the cartoon as well as the language that went with it. It is important that the pictures or drawings include language so that children like Owen learn more than what he looks like in the visual – he learns what the language means that goes with his choices of behavior. In order for Owen and others with ASD to learn the social concepts of behavior so that they can choose prosocial ways to function, they must acquire the Language of Pictures. The Language of Pictures may be the shape of the written word that makes mental visuals for some students, like Owen. In this way, they learn a vision of social thinking.

Owen arrived at therapy ... still talking about being scared, having cried at school, being mad at his "best friend" Ronaldo due to something that had happened at least two hours ago at school. As Owen was headed to the bathroom to pee, Ronaldo stopped him and told him there was a "Big, green monster in the boys' bathroom!" Owen (chose) to become scared, to cry, to tattle to the teacher, and to act grumpy and feel sorry for himself. Owen chose to act like a bad sport. Owen tattled on his friend, Ronaldo. Ronaldo did not do anything wrong, so he will wonder why Owen tattled on him. Ronaldo might decide that Owen is not his friend.

In therapy, I drew out the situation at school, but drew Owen as <u>part of the problem</u> ... not the victim!

Owen created a problem when he believed there was a monster ... we talked about monsters being pretend and unable to hurt you ... fear of a nonexistent object is irrational!

Owen chose to cry and become afraid. Owen chose not to walk into the bathroom. Therefore, Owen chose not to go potty in the toilet. Owen chose to feel pain in his bladder. Owen chose to tattle to the teacher. Owen chose to take the teacher's time away from the other 25 students who were waiting for her while she took Owen to the bathroom. Owen's classmates were upset with Owen for taking up the teacher's teaching time while they waited.

Solution:

Owen doesn't have to cry or be scared. Owen doesn't have to hold his pee in his bladder. Owen doesn't have to tattle to the teacher. Owen doesn't have to take time away from the other students.

Owen could laugh at Ronaldo's joke. Owen could make his own joke. Owen could play along with the joking around! Owen could "tease" Ronaldo about the monster too! When Owen chooses to act like a good sport, he is also choosing to act like a friend toward Ronaldo. Ronaldo will respect Owen because Owen knows how to take a joke and laugh with his friend, Ronaldo.

Figure 6.14. **Owen needs more writing than drawing to see the meaning of the language.**

Activity: Why does higher-order thinking used to understand concepts like friendship or consideration require the use of multiple visuals over-lapped with written language that explains the visuals?

By helping a child act in prosocial or antisocial ways, the child's caregivers and educators are also helping the child determine whether or not his social development (e.g., Buron, 2007) will be prosocial or antisocial. The better the child understands society's rules for behavior, the better the child is able to develop his own social determination. For example, a child diagnosed with Asperger Syndrome may test as having a genius IQ, but the same child may not understand that he is not the "commander" of other people's behavior.

Andrew is a case in point. At 6 years of age, Andrew is very capable of telling the adults around him what to do, "Hang your jacket with the sleeves down. Sleeves on the edge of the hanger means sleeves don't stretch." Over and over, Andrew told the teacher to straighten the desks, arrange the books on the table, clear the tables, and so on. He often used adult-like language similar to the coat hanger example and even explained his rationale for why he wanted the teacher to line up the edges of the paper, create neat piles of dust when sweeping, and so on. The adults around Andrew marveled at his "brightness" and even thought his rule orders were "cute." However, many other people thought his nonstop verbal commands were annoying. His parents explained, "Andrew is too smart. He just needs some social skills."

As Andrew continued to grow, his annoying behavior of telling others what to do irritated both teachers and peers. Students did not like to work with him because he insisted on running the format of the activity, often at the expense of the quality of work. When his parents signed him up for music, no one wanted to share a music stand with him because he would stop playing his clarinet to arrange the music, affecting the other person's ability to read the music. Students did not invite Andrew to join them in play or other activities because he had also developed the excuses to go with the telling of others what to do, "Hang up your coat. I am smart and I will tell you what to do. Take your books and put them on the table ..."

Andrew had learned how to use a basic antisocial way of interacting with others. He had not learned how to use his gift of being smart to become prosocial. Even though he was "smart," he was not socially smart. A socially smart person would understand that others do not like to be "micro-managed." His social behavior was that of a 3- to 7-year-old child; that is, preoperational in nature. Andrew needed teachers and family members to assign prosocial meaning to his behavior so that he did not perpetuate antisocial ways of "being smart." He needed lots of concepts drawn and written about so that he would develop the concepts he was missing.

Figure 6.15 shows the Language of Pictures of how to become a "team member." This example shows how Andrew wants to "fit into society" at a concrete level but how he is socially still at a preoperational level. The reciprocal interaction in writing and drawing between the therapist and Andrew is a way to assign the meaning of the concept "team member."

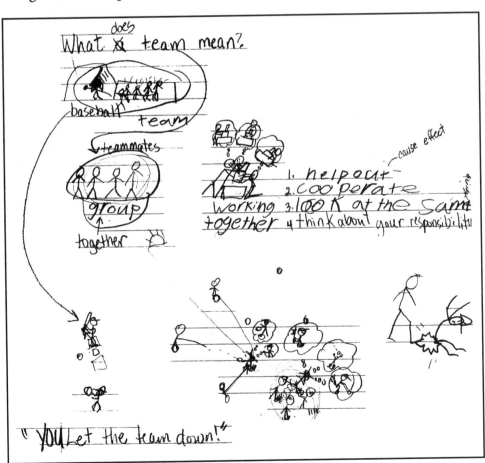

Figure 6.15. **Andrew draws his ideas.**

Notice how Andrew draws symbolized icons of what he does. In other words, down at the bottom of the figure he draws himself alone on separate tasks. Andrew does not have the Language of Pictures necessary to understand that the prosocial behavior of being a team player or working on a team means that there are other people in his pictures. In order for Andrew to develop this type of prosocial behavior, he needed these types of messages when he was very young so that he could learn (a) what he looked like to others; (b) what his words meant to others; and (c) what others thought when they wanted to interact or play games with him instead of sorting the checkers, and so forth. In other words, Andrew needed the adults to assign a prosocial meaning to his behavior and correct his antisocial behavior so that he could learn how to be prosocial. Without the prosocial meaning, he had excuses for acting inappropriately.

Activity: In any given situation, a person can act prosocially or antisocially. Why?

Andrew attended speech therapy for social skills work every year, but he did not improve because he added the new behaviors or skills to concepts that were antisocial in nature. For example, he learned to shake hands when he met people, so every time his friend's mom came to school, Andrew walked over to her and said, "Hello, my name is Andrew." He shook hands and then said, "It is nice to meet you." This may look prosocial, but it is not.

These words are inappropriate and do not add to the development of the social relationship between his friend's mom and Andrew, since they already have met and know each other. A prosocial behavior would be something like, "Hello … it is good to see you again! Are you and Peter (his friend) going to the baseball game this weekend?" This last set of ideas would continue the development of the social relationship. Figures 6.16-6.18 show other concepts that Andrew must also learn in order to develop sufficient meaning about "team work" to be able to function prosocially on a team.

Figure 6.16. **Drawing new concepts.**

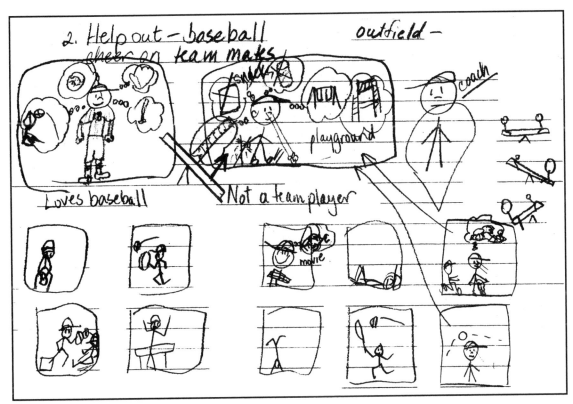

Figure 6.17. Learning the meaning of new concepts.

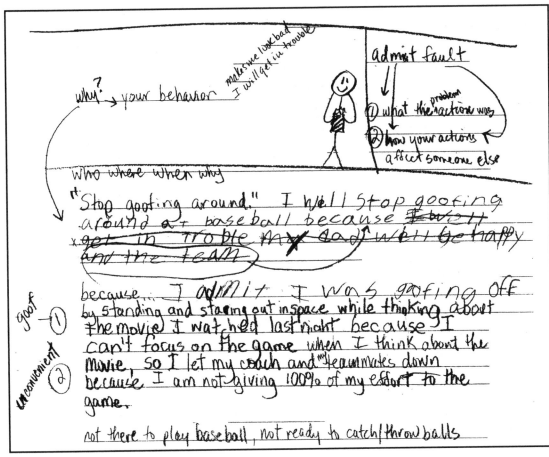

Figure 6.18. Writing about new concepts.

It is important for the parents and educators of a child with ASD to determine what type of social development they want. Do they want to develop skills with or without the underlying prosocial understanding? Or do they want to always work on prosocial concepts? If the latter is their choice, they need to be sure they help the child determine his or her social reason for acting in relationship to others in the child's environment. Social conceptual development requires the Language of Pictures to develop prosocial behavior. In this way, the social determination of the child is positive, and the child is more likely to develop social competence. The child learns the Language of Pictures about being socially competent.

Activity: What is social determination?

Social Competence

The ultimate learning goal for most parents is for their children to become socially competent. ***Social competence refers to the ability to initiate and maintain healthy social relationships.*** Healthy relationships improve an individual's success at school, at work, in the community, and in the family. Furthermore, healthy relationships help a person's overall well-being and life satisfaction.

To initiate healthy relationships, a child must be able to communicate basic needs in relationship to what others can provide. This means that the adults in the child's life must assign prosocial meaning to what the child does, even at a very early age. For example, when a child screams, the parent has choices for how to respond. The parent can try to stop the child from screaming by using a verbal punishment such as, "No, stop screaming. I do not like it when you scream." But these words do not provide the child with a mental picture of what others think when the child screams. It is important that the child's Language of Pictures include other people, if the child is to develop social concepts. Having other people in the child's pictures means that the child is at a societal, concrete level of understanding rules, able to make choices that are, by societal standards, acceptable. In this way, the child is learning to socially think with a vision of what others think.

Another choice would be to remove the screaming child from the setting. By being removed from the setting, the child is prevented from interacting with others in the setting, which may have been the antisocial behavior the child wanted. But without language explaining why he was removed, the only concept the child learns is that screaming behavior removes you from unwanted input. To develop the Language of Pictures for social competence, the child needs to *see* what he does, in this case screaming, that affects others' pictures and thoughts. The child needs to *see* how his behavior of screaming affects other people's dinner, work, TV watching, or ride on the school bus. Again, for the child to learn to develop the social concepts of how the child functions in relationship to others, the child needs the Language of Pictures to learn how he becomes part of the event and how he relates to others in a prosocial way.

For example, an adolescent, Dennis, wanted to play video games every time he climbed into a car. When his dad offered a friend a ride, Dennis played with the video games. The friend said he did not want to be in the car because Dennis ignored him. Dennis was disappointed that his friend did not want to ride with him.

Figure 6.19 (a and b) shows how Dennis drew and wrote about the various relationships of the situation. These relationships include how Dennis relates to other people (agents) such as his dad and his friend; how Dennis relates to their actions (what) such as riding or driving the car, how Dennis relates to the place of the event (where) such as being in the same space of the car together, and why and how friends want to share the space of the car. Through these drawings and writings, Dennis is learning about being a friend in the car. He is learning about the effects of his behavior on others, and he is learning that there are "others" in his pictures. In Figure 6.19a, notice that he starts out writing about his game with his dad and how nobody else knows about the game. Also, notice that he never thinks about teaching the game to his friend. He only has a vision of thinking that relates him to his game. He sees the game. Dennis does not realize that no one else can see the video game.

Figure 6.19a. **The car game.**

A child who learns how others influence him and how his behavior affects others acquires more language to help develop social competence. The path to social competence means the child's behavior must be more prosocial, which will also provide opportunities for more independent living. The visuals used for developing social competence include people, their actions, and their consequences, all within a story or event (Arwood & Unruh, 2000) of how to look and behave with what others think. Eventually, Dennis draws some solution types of behaviors for what he could do in the car when he is with other people, like his mom or Terry, who do not know what the "car game" is.

Figure 6.19b. **Talking about something other than the car game.**

Many children, like those diagnosed with ASD, do not know that they are making sound with their hands, feet, and mouths that others can hear. They know they are moving their fingers, feet, or lips, but they do not process the sound and, therefore, do not know why others tell them "Be quiet," "Stop moving," and so on. From an antisocial perspective, a person who "drums' with his fingers might even see another person's annoyance as that person's problem, as opposed to a problem with the drumming. In Figure 6.20, a preadolescent is shown the visual Language of Pictures about how "finger drumming" affects others.

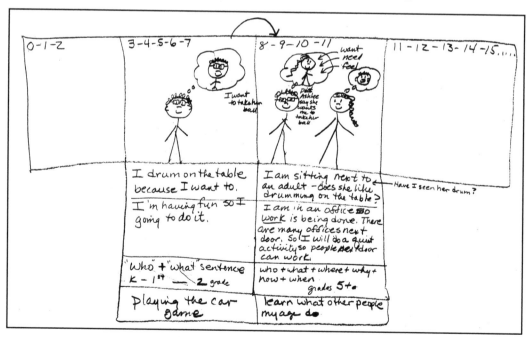

Figure 6.20. **Finger drumming.**

All children, including those who are not diagnosed with ASD, need the social language of their behavior to be able to act appropriately. For example, a beginning first-grade teacher instructed her students on the way to the bathroom, "Reach out and touch the wall. That is how close I want you to be to the wall. So, when we walk down the hallway, stay this (she reached out and touched the wall with her hand and with her foot to illustrate) close to the wall." As soon as the teacher began to walk, the students reached out and touched the wall the way she had told them to do. Each child struggled to touch the wall with his or her hand and foot walking down the hall. Needless to say, the students were very slow walking down the hall.

This new teacher walked ahead of the line. When she arrived at the bathroom and turned around, the teacher was surprised to see the students only half way there. The students were struggling to get under a heating duct that protruded out of the wall while still touching the wall with their hands and their feet. Most of the first graders were too tall to walk vertically under the duct while still touching the wall with their hands and with their feet.

The teacher was baffled at the children's clumsy, slow behavior, and turned to the author and said, "What are they doing?" The author responded, "They are doing exactly what you told them to do." She thought about the words and then laughed. "I told them to stay close to the wall and then showed them what 'close' meant by touching the wall with my hand and foot. They thought they were to imitate what I did. They did not know what I meant by 'stay close' even though I showed them."

This example illustrates how neurotypical learners also struggle to acquire the language of what they see. The teacher's hand movements created a picture that did not match the nuances of the social meaning of her words. This means that the teacher (Arwood, Brown, & Robb, 2005; Arwood & Robb, 2008) must use more spoken language with her hand movement of touching the wall so she can create the language of the social concepts for the children. For example, "When you walk down the hall, I want to see your hands at your side like this, your eyes on the person's head in front of you, and your mouths closed so that the words do not fall out of your mouth and fill the space of children in nearby rooms." If the teacher does not give more language but decides to punish students who don't comply by rewarding others for "good walking," she will increase the children's antisocial behavior, because each child will learn to work against the good of others in order to get the reward. For example, she could say to one child, "Sarah, I like the way you are walking." But, there are other children who are also walking and they do not have a mental picture of how they look compared to Sarah. As a result of this type of language, the children who do not understand how Sarah looks different than they do may feel punished.

Research shows that punishment[7] increases aggressiveness in children, which for many people ultimately turns into violence (Walker, Ramsey, & Gresham, 2004). In order to ensure that prosocial behavior leads to social competence (not violence), all individuals need positive meaning given to their behavior in a story of language that assigns meaning to the social concepts.

The Language of Pictures for developing social competence begins in the earliest stages. For example, a first-grade student with ASD would not work in therapy because he had left the video that he was to watch after therapy in his mother's car. Since he could not "see" the video, he could not understand the situation. When the language of the situation was drawn for him (see Figure 6.21), he was able to understand Mom's oral language about the video.

---

7   Punishment, by definition, temporarily stops an unwanted behavior. But all rewards are punishers, and all punishers are rewards. For example, a child who receives a reward for doing a good job in P.E. may wonder why he works hard on other days but does not receive a reward on those days. Likewise, other children in P.E. who think they work hard but do not receive the reward may feel punished.

Figure 6.21. **I see myself and my sack.**

He had developed the Language of Pictures, so he "knew" he and his mom had picked up a video but they had left it in the car when he went into therapy. He did not have the language for when he was to use the video, even though his mom had orally told him. In Figure 6.22, drawing the meaning of Mom's oral language provides him with what he will look like when he is finished with therapy and once again has the video tape that he picked up at the grocery store.

Figure 6.22. **I see myself riding home holding my sack.**

Summary

Social skills are products of the learning system. So, when adults make visuals about social skills, the visuals are abstract pictures showing a product of learning such as "shaking hands" out of context. The adult uses these types of visuals because the adult assumes that the child understands the words that define the social skill. For example, "shaking hands" is a phrase of two words that defines what a person does with her hands that is referred to as shaking hands (product of the learning system). If the child with ASD does not see herself in relationship to others and others' actions, she will not be able to understand the meaning of "shaking hands" unless the action is put into an event. Remember that an event consists of people who do actions within a context that relates to the learner. So, the child with ASD must understand the relationship between her and the act of "shaking hands:" When do you shake hands? Why do you shake hands? Who shakes hands? And so forth. To really understand the social skill of shaking hands, the child needs more pictures about the concepts that underlie what it means to shake hands. Figure 6.23 shows this type of pictured social skill.

Figure 6.23. **Shaking hands with a person.**

The situation in Figure 6.24 is even more difficult. It is a symbolic picture without the relationships of who, when, where, how, or why to shake hands. The hands are not even part of a person.

Figure 6.24. **Shaking hands, the formal concept.**

To learn the underlying concepts of social skills, a child must develop the Language of Pictures for acquisition of social concepts. In this way, the child gains a vision of how to think about being social. Learning how one's behavior affects others' acts and how to choose to change behavior so as to be socially competent requires multiple layers of pictures, as shown in Figures 6.15-6.18. These multiple overlapping sets of pictures connect the language to the pictures to form visual mental concepts of what "prosocial" behavior looks like as determined by societal expectations. In this way, a child learns to be socially competent.

Chapter 7 will explain how the journey of the Language of Pictures includes the content of the curriculum.

CHAPTER 7
Visuals in the Curriculum

Seeing the idea come alive is more than a picture ...
It is a movement of patterns put to music
And sung to the change of colors.
It is the picture of what others think as well as what I know.

All concepts can be put into a graphic ... even those that represent formal, abstract ideas such as liberty, justice, love, respect, health, government, and so forth. It is important to remember that all graphics are representations of someone's perception. And all perceptions come from our sensory input. Sensory input is unique to each individual. Each person receives the sensory input from his or her environment. Each environment is different, so all input is unique.

This unique sensory input interconnects to form patterns of perception. Since the sensory input is unique, all perceptions are unique and, therefore, valid. This does not mean people agree or disagree or even like each other's perception. It just means that the learning system provides each person with unique patterns of perception. These perceptions are grouped into systems of concepts, so concepts or thinking consist of unique perceptions. Concepts are represented by the patterns of a language, which, in turn, represent unique underlying conceptualization. As concept development increases, so does the complexity of thinking. Most curricula aim at teaching increasingly more complex concepts.

The purpose of this chapter is to show why and how the use of visuals in the curriculum is important for developing higher-order thinking and problem solving.

Power of the Language of Pictures

For two or more people to be able to communicate their unique ideas between and among themselves, common patterns of representation must be formed. For example, people who share English patterns sequence sounds to form the word "table" to refer to a flat object used for putting plates on. So when one person thinks of the concept "table," he thinks of the table where his mom put the dishes. Because he is looking down on the table from his mind's eye (Jensen, 1998), he sees the table from that perspective. When asked to draw his concept of table, he draws the table as if he were on top of the table, so his drawing looks like Figure 7.1.

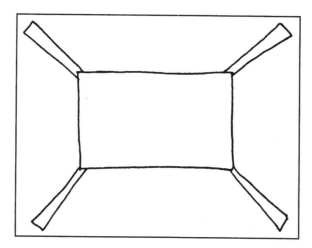

Figure 7.1. **An over-the-top perspective of table.**

The other person's sister spent time in New Mexico; her drawing of the concept "table" looks like Figure 7.2.

Figure 7.2. **A table is a flat-topped mountain.**

These two individuals, with similar family backgrounds, and both speakers of English, drew the same concept, "table," but they produced two different drawings. The notion that the same language term consists of different underlying conceptual meanings is a result of the unique underlying experiences that result in differences of meaning. ***Because these unique meanings form concepts that language represents, language holds lots of power in the many meanings of each concept.***

Activity: Why can two people have different perceptions of the same concept or word?

Knowing that thinking consists of perceptual patterns that make up the concepts for language helps us understand why using oral language results in many misperceptions and misconceptions. For example, a ninth-grade, award-winning physical science teacher was loved by many students. He was considered one of the best teachers by his colleagues, parents, and students in the community.

The students were quite successful at repeating the "patterns" of words the teacher gave them. For example, they loved playing "Jeopardy" in class. When given the answer "A natural place for ground water," most of the students could quickly give the question "What is a water shed?" The students had learned the definition in science: "A water shed is a natural place for ground water." The teacher also provided many opportunities to give the students the memorized word patterns through multiple-choice, fill-in-the blank, crossword-puzzle types of tests. Students could easily say or match the words they memorized.

Class was fun, and students appeared to be understanding the concepts taught. But even though the students liked the teacher, a fairly significant percentage of them struggled academically. One of the authors asked the teacher to have all his students draw what they thought a "water shed" was, in an attempt to see if they truly understood the concepts taught. This activity was done at the end of nine weeks focusing on the concept "water shed," after the students had already taken the final exam covering the concept. The nine-week unit consisted of hands-on experiments, practice with terminology such as the Jeopardy games or crossword puzzles, completing lots of worksheets in cooperative learning groups, a couple of field trips, movies, and textbook reading.

The teacher was reluctant to add one more activity, but he agreed to have the students draw their conceptualization of "water shed" at the end of the unit. Out of the more than 120 students he had in several physical science sections, only 3 drew anything that closely represented the notion that a "water shed" is not a building but the term for an underground storage of water from run-off. Figures 7. 3 and 7.4 show examples of what most students drew.

Figure 7.3. **A water shed is a shed that catches water.**

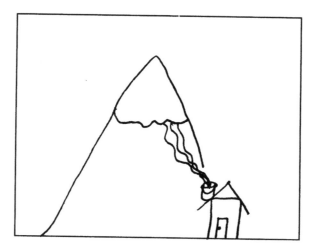

Figure 7.4. **A water shed is a catch basin for a mountain.**

Activity: Why were the students not learning, even though the teacher provided good teaching?

The teacher was dumbfounded! In fact, he was so surprised that he thought the students were joking. To find out what had happened, he asked individual students to explain what they had drawn. The students earnestly explained how the water collects in a building-like shed to be used later. The teacher asked them how the water collects, and they responded that it collects when it rains. Some had the shed at the base of a mountain to show how the run-off from the mountain would fall into the shed (see Figure 7.4)

To probe further, the teacher pulled out the graphic of a water shed in the students' textbook (see Figure 7.5) and asked some of the students about it. The students had read the material from the book in class. They had also discussed this graphic and had had many opportunities to apply their knowledge so they should be able to understand the conceptual meaning of the graphic. The teacher asked, "So how does this water shed compare with the one you drew?"

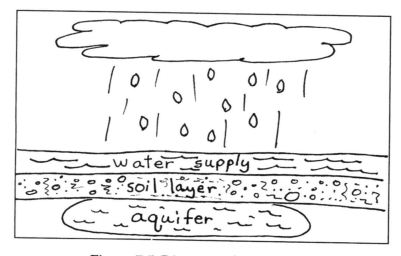

Figure 7.5. **Diagram of water shed.**

Visual Thinking Strategies
142

The students responded that his graphic showed the dirt, gravel, and so on, under the soil and that they had drawn the water shed. The students did not understand that the "underground soil and rocks were representative of a water shed." It was apparent that the graphic was not at the appropriate cognitive level (see Chapters 2, 3, and 4) for these high school students. For nine weeks, the students had a mental picture of what a water shed was, and all of the activities in class had not helped them refine that mental picture into the concept they were studying. But asking the students to draw their understanding of the concept resulted in the students drawing what they knew, which allowed the teacher to see the difference between his understanding of the concept and the students' understanding of the concept. *Visuals are used in the curriculum to help give a picture of the language about concepts as well as to help students learn the full meaning of a formal or abstract concept.* In this way, there is a lot of learning power in the Language of Pictures.

Activity: Why does a student's drawing tell the teacher what the student understands?

Matching Concepts to Language

In the example about water shed, the students could produce the phrase "water shed." They could do experiments about the term and even match patterns from class and the text on a test. However, they did not understand the full meaning of the concept. Remember that concepts develop over time. So the majority of these students knew that a "water shed" collected water, which means they had a concrete understanding of what a water shed is about. But pitchers, bottles, bathtubs, all collect water. And they knew what a shed looks like … So they literally drew something like a shed that collected water. They did not possess the formal understanding of the concept water shed, a natural underground place for run off water.

To understand a formal concept, students need to represent their meaning and then have the teacher or another person give feedback. Drawing in real time provides students with an authentic opportunity to represent their ideas about a concept, and the teacher can help add meaning by writing and drawing in response. This additional visual meaning refines the basic conceptualization into more formal concepts.

To create a shared Language of Pictures, both the teacher and the students must draw concepts. A fifth-grade teacher, Alyse Rostamizadeh (Mrs. R), draws for all of her students in addition to drawing for individual students who might be struggling. Mrs. R took textbook questions and rephrased them into a single question that she wrote for a student who was struggling. Figure 7. 6 shows what she wrote.

Name three ways in which water can change the earth.

Figure 7.6. **Write out the ideas to begin to form the Language of Pictures.**

The student, who is on the spectrum, could read the question fluently but did not understand it. So Mrs. R. drew the meaning of the question.

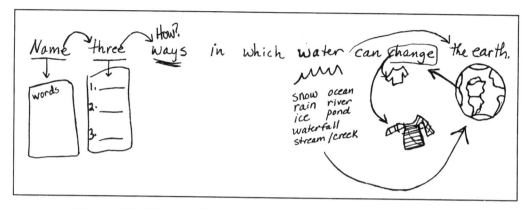

Figure 7.7. **The teacher draws the meaning of the sentence.**

The student drew what he knew based on what the teacher drew. Figure 7.8 shows the student's drawing.

Figure 7.8. **One student's perception of the way water changes the earth.**

Notice that in Figure 7.8, the student is thinking of one way that the earth changes as a result of rain. This is a single-picture level of understanding, or a preoperational level of understanding. In other words, the student has some meaning but not the multiple meanings that the original question requested. The student was subsequently asked to draw out the steps of what happens when it rains and to write the words with the drawings. In this way, the student is learning that multiple pictures are needed to answer the question. Figure 7.9 shows what he wrote and drew.

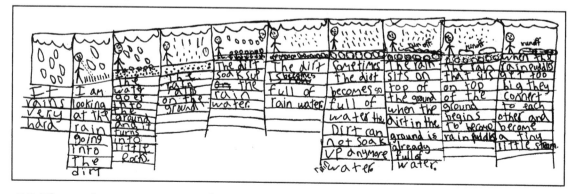

Figure 7.9. **The student cartoons out the science process of what happens to the earth when it rains.**

Figures 7.10-7.14 are notes from Mrs. R's lessons on electromagnetic waves. She draws out her ideas and then draws ideas in class for the students.

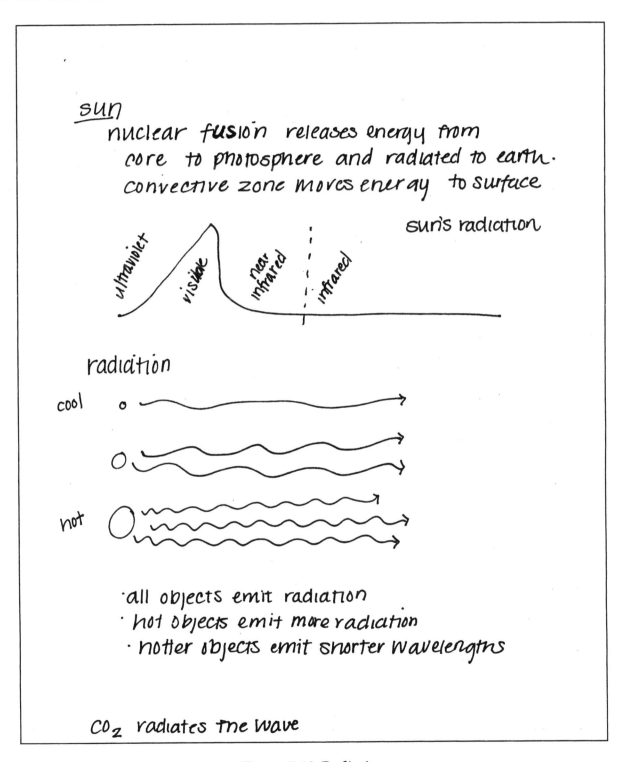

Figure 7.10. **Radiation.**

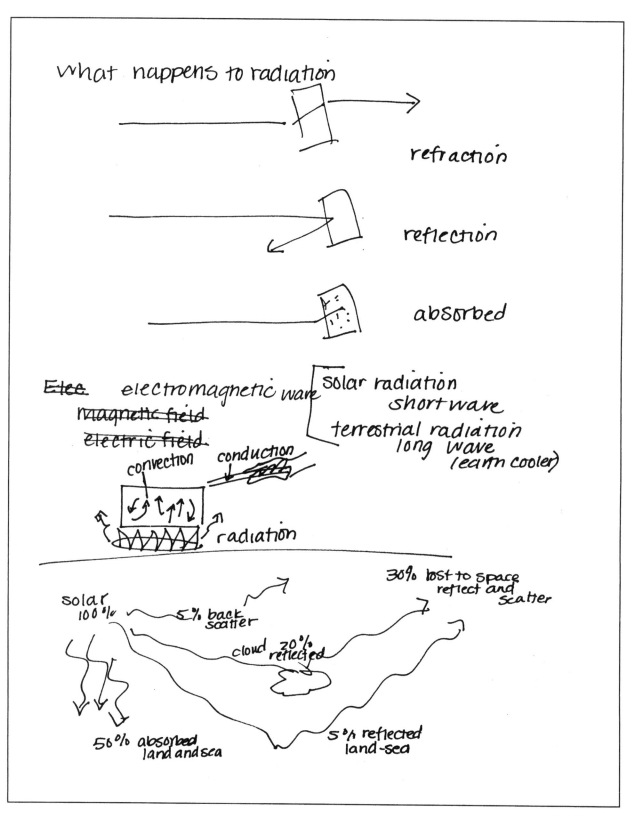

Figure 7.11. **What happens to radiation.**

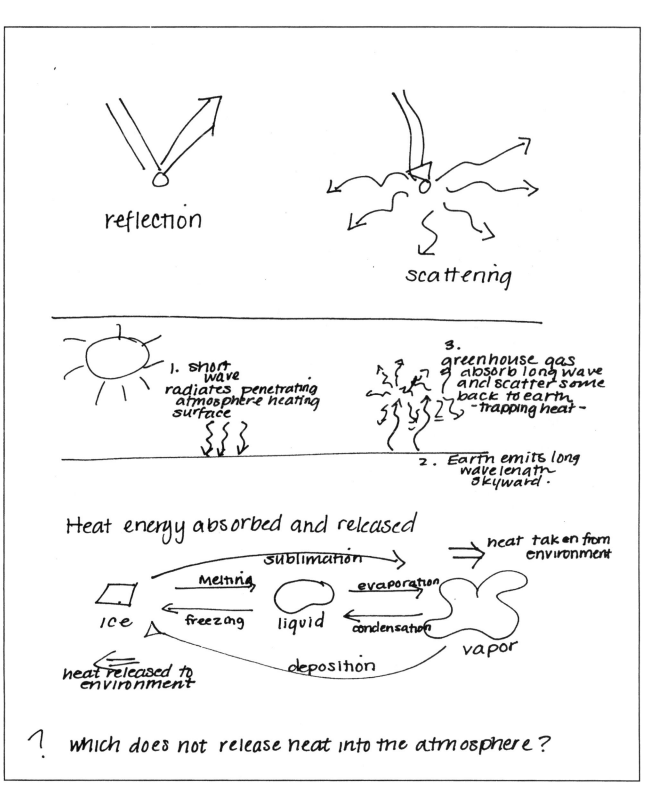

reflection

scattering

1. short wave radiates penetrating atmosphere heating surface

3. greenhouse gas absorb long wave and scatter some back to earth -trapping heat-

2. Earth emits long wavelength skyward.

Heat energy absorbed and released

heat taken from environment

sublimation

melting

evaporation

ice   liquid   vapor

freezing   condensation

heat released to environment

deposition

? which does not release heat into the atmosphere?

Figure 7.12. Heat energy absorbed.

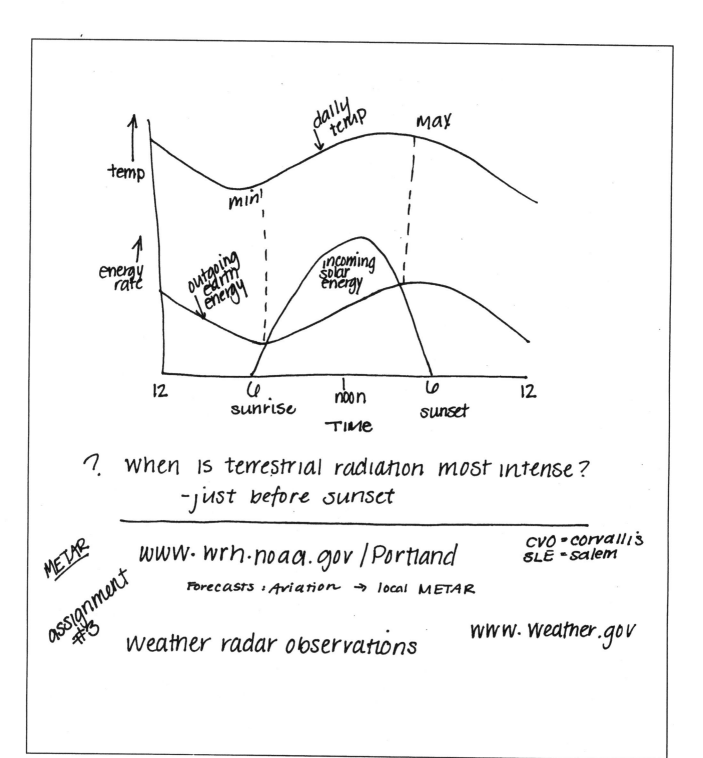

? when is terrestrial radiation most intense?
— just before sunset

METAR

assignment #3

www.wrh.noaa.gov/Portland

Forecasts: Aviation → local METAR

weather radar observations

CVO = corvallis
SLE = salem

www.weather.gov

Figure 7.13. Terrestrial radiation.

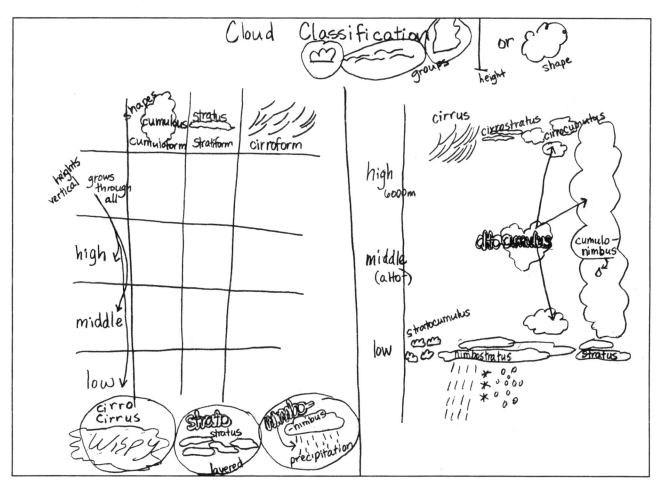

Figure 7.14. **Cloud classification.**

This type of drawing in the classroom helps students with autism spectrum disorders (ASD) to remain in the general education classroom and develop strategies for their use in understanding concepts, like those for reading (Gately, 2008). Because students with ASD use a motor access to concepts, many will not do their own drawings. They will let the teacher draw and then they will write. If the teacher is drawing for all of the students, others will also benefit, as demonstrated by the example of the water changes on the earth. Most of the students think in a visual set of language pictures that requires the classroom teacher to create the Language of Pictures of the concepts being acquired. For example, one student did not write (see Figure 7.15), but once she learned that she could draw what she knew, she was able to write (see Figure 7.16).

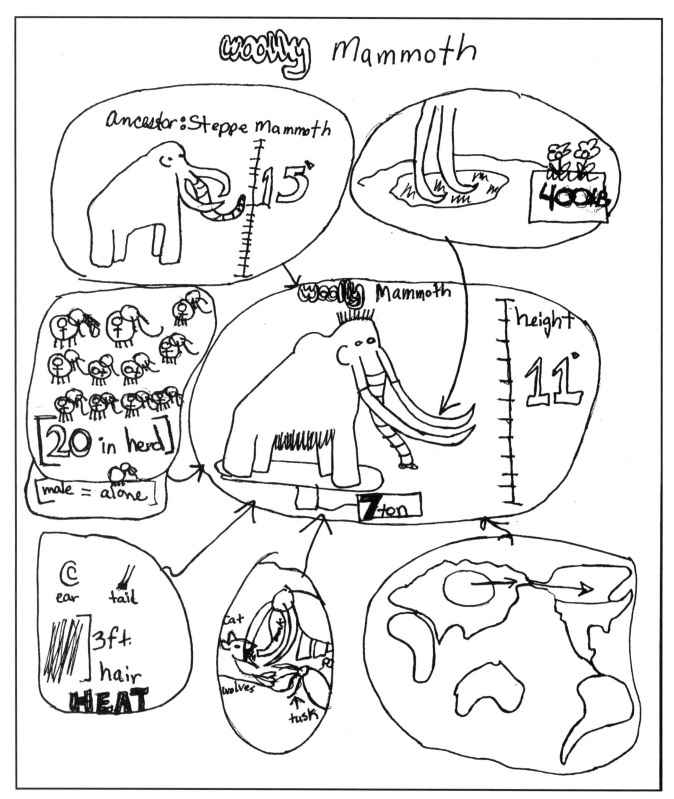

Figure 7.15. **Some students can draw their ideas and are able to use the drawings as their language so they can write.**

The drawing provides the concepts for the student, whereas the writing provides the language that represents the drawing or pictures.

Once on the frozen ~~tundra~~ lived the woolly Mammoth. They moved from Northern asia, and migrated to north america. The woolly mammoths ancestor was named the steppe Mammoth. The steppe was about 4 feet taller than the mammoth, which was an average of eleven feet. Their large bodies were covered with 3 feet of long hair, short tails, and small ears to help them preserve the heat. The Woolly Mammoth used its long, curved ~~tusks~~ to scrape the ice and snow off the green foolage. The woolly mammoth would graze as they travel from place to place, and would eat about 400 pounds of food a day.

Figure 7.16. Once the student has drawn her pictures, she has the power of those pictures to write her ideas.

The power of the drawn concepts comes from the notion that drawings are conceptual; that is, representations of understanding. What we draw, we know. So when the teacher draws, the teacher must know her subject matter and must be able to represent the meaning in a variety of pictures to give students the full language of the concepts being learned. As the students acquire the Language of the Pictures the teacher draws, they are learning the formal concepts in the curriculum, not just giving back the patterns of fun activities, as in the case of the physical science teacher we met earlier.

Activity: Why does drawing in a curriculum help students learn concepts? Why does drawing in the classroom create the Language of Pictures?

Guideposts for Classroom Drawing

- Drawings of concepts represent perceptions. Therefore, there are no right or wrong drawings.

- Drawings of curriculum concepts are not artwork. The visuals represent meaning.

- Drawings of concepts occur in real time. The teacher, parent, or clinician draws his or her understanding of a concept while also talking about it. The student, especially a student with ASD, watches the movement of the hand, thereby seeing how the concept forms a graphic.

- Movement of the hand creates meaning; the finished product does not necessarily provide the same meaning.

- Looking at a drawing that represents someone else's ideas may not have any meaning to the person looking.

- Some low-functioning children with ASD look to the side or don't look up at all while another person is drawing, especially when the adult takes the child's hand and moves it (H/H) at the same time as the adult draws. Remember: The child obtains more information from the shape of the movement than from what the drawing looks like. Therefore, the child may not want to look at the writing but instead looks away from the hand in order to feel the movement of the hand.

- Many, if not most, children and adults with ASD do not draw. They use the written print of language to represent what they know. They use others' drawings to gain meaning or conceptualization and the written language to match their meanings to the drawing. Writing or printed words are easier to see as shapes whereas each person draws a concept with a different shape. So, often a person with ASD will write and the adult will assign meaning to the child's writing by drawing the meaning of what the child wrote. Rewriting or redrawing the differences in meaning between writing and drawing helps add conceptual meaning.

- While the teacher draws or talks, a student diagnosed with ASD who has an assistant needs the assistant to translate the classroom curriculum into drawings that have the written words matched to the pictures.

- Any type of movement of the pencil on the paper, drawing on the dry-erase board, drawing of concepts on paper, and so on, creates meaning for the child to use.

- Different levels of drawing represent different levels of understanding of concepts.

- Drawings are not conventional[8], because they represent the unique properties of perception that form concepts. Therefore, drawings do not represent language. The Language of Pictures comes from attaching the words or symbols to the concepts or drawings; in other words, they answer the question: What do the pictures mean?

Activity: *What are some of the guideposts about drawing to create concepts in the classroom?*

---

8 In language, the term "conventional" refers to the shared meaning that a symbol would have for two or more people. For example, "table" is a word that most English speakers share. Therefore, "table" is a conventional word. But people do not draw the same picture to a shared word. So when adults are asked to draw their meaning of "table," they draw many unique pictures of different kinds of tables. Thus, pictures or drawings are not conventional.

Developing the Curriculum from the Language of Pictures

Academic curricula consist of a sequence of developing concepts. For example, in first grade, students learn about how an animal lives. In second grade students learn about different types of animals and their lives. By third grade, students are learning to categorize animals by their living characteristics. By fourth grade, students are learning about how animals and plants are not the same in the way that they live. And by fifth grade, students are learning about the characteristics of different niches and their relationship to geography and climate changes.

Since children and adults with ASD think in visual graphics that are often developed from the movement of the mouth, the hands, the pencil on paper, the fingers for signing, and so on, it is important to recognize that there are multiple motor ways to develop mental visual graphics. But if a person with ASD needs to use movement to create concepts, his production of patterns is not the same as his understanding of concepts. For example, an adolescent diagnosed with high-functioning autism, Miguel, can orally read an age-appropriate textbook, can speak in front of large audiences about what it means to have autism, and can participate in fine arts activities at his high school, but his understanding of a lot of concepts is significantly below age level. In other words, he is able to produce patterns that others interpret as his understanding, but in reality he lacks significant meaning of many concepts.

Figure 7.17 provides an example of some of the concepts that Miguel has worked on for the last couple of years to begin to bridge his learned patterns with conceptual meaning. The teacher draws the concepts, and Miguel does the writing. Since this student learns best from the motor movements, the writing is edited to match the meaning of the drawn concepts. That is, he learns to match his mental pictures or concepts to the language patterns of the meanings. In this way, he learns the concepts of the Language of Pictures.

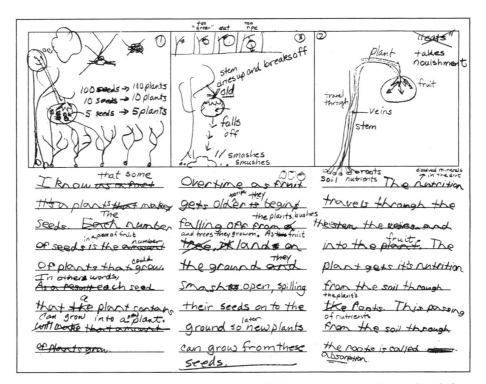

Figure 7.17. **Miguel learns that plants "come" from seeds, not from bird droppings.**

Because Miguel needs to be able to see the motor movement of the hand to create differences in shapes, many of the concepts about seeds are drawn as shapes of bubbles matched to the written patterns. The written bubbles are shapes of language that matches the drawn concepts. Figure 7.18 shows some of these concepts.

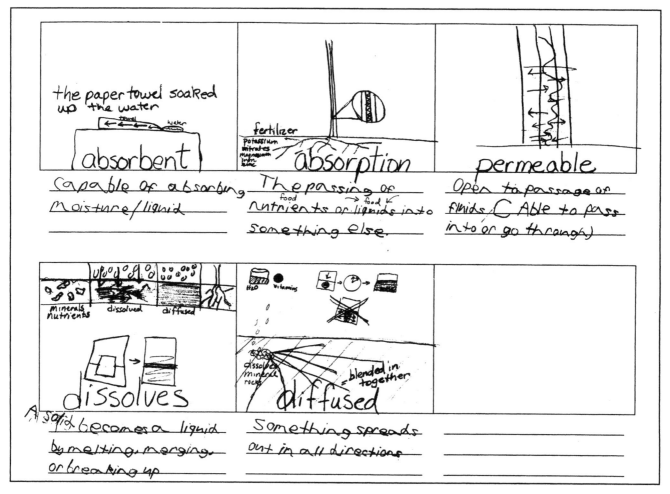

Figure 7.18. **Miguel learns the meaning of some of the similar word patterns.**

Eventually, the written patterns and pictures are connected into a flowchart type of graphic. This flowchart graphic provides multiple sets of meanings related to where plants come from. Figure 7.19 is an example of some of the many meanings that were connected for this adolescent. (Remember that multiple visuals are needed to develop concepts.) As the academic or social concepts become more complex, the individual learning the concepts needs more and more visuals to connect the meaning among concepts. By connecting multiple sets of concepts, the learner acquires more conceptual meaning of the Language of Pictures.

For a neurotypical learner, the sound of a caregiver's or teacher's voice provides the language for what the learner sees in the book, on the chalk board, or around the room. Note that the student with ASD represented in Figures 7.17-7.19 learned from writing with the pictures first and then matching the pictures to the writing. The writing is the language for the pictures, which are the concepts.

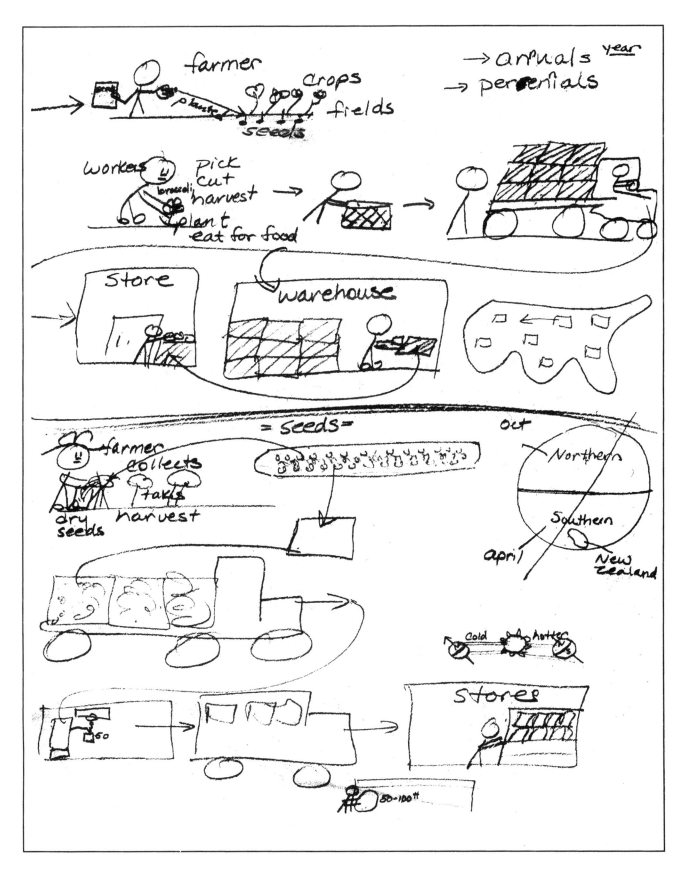

Figure 7.19. Miguel is learning how the pictures of the concepts relate to language.

If you as a reader are looking at some of these graphics, like the flowchart, and you are thinking that these drawings don't make sense, remember that the "sense" or meaning comes from the drawing being accomplished in real time. During real-time drawing, the student is watching the movements of the hand to create mental visual shapes of ideas. In this way, the meaning is from the process, not the product. These graphics are a process, whereas you are looking at the product of someone else's language, not your language.

Finally, the student in Figures 7.17 through 7.19 goes back to the way he learns best and writes out what he has learned from matching the drawings to the writing movements. Figure 7.20 shows the writing that goes with the flowchart in Figure 7.19.

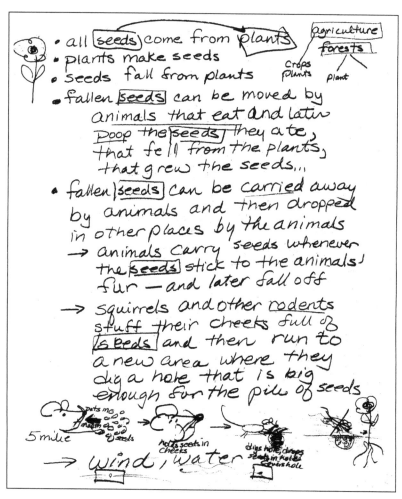

Figure 7.20. **Miguel's own language matched to the pictures.**

The match of writing words to the drawn concepts yielded a significant increase in this student's ability to follow the academic curriculum, in addition to a statistically significant increase in his IQ score as well as noticeable differences reported by others about his oral language and his ability to function socially with others.

Activity: Why does providing a student with the Language of Pictures help increase his conceptualization?

Patterns Versus Concepts in the Curriculum

Students are often asked to respond to the teacher's questions or to test questions with patterns of what the teacher says, what the book says, what the worksheet says, and so on. In other words, educators often encourage students to imitate, copy, and repeat patterns from other sources such as the teacher, the book, or the worksheet. The assumption is that the students will be able to turn these patterns into their own concepts. And, it is true … students who can bring their own language to the curriculum are able to put language to the patterns and, therefore, develop meaning from the patterns to increase their conceptualization. But students on the autism spectrum are not able to make the academic patterns into concepts unless they can bring their own visual mental graphics to the situation. These visual mental graphics increase from single pictures and images to more related pictures that eventually form multiple mental movies.

When a person is able to create a visual mental movie about a concept, she has enough language to convert the academic patterns in the curriculum to the Language of Pictures. It is the authors' experiences with children and adults on the autism spectrum that most of these individuals are able to repeat and produce the academic patterns but do not have a concrete or formal understanding of many academic, even everyday, concepts.

Because educators often emphasize the production of patterns, it is very possible for students with ASD to make it through the curriculum of school with a huge number of patterns but with little conceptualization. If a student reaches young adulthood able to primarily use patterns but unable to think with concepts, the student will not be able to live alone. Someone else will have to provide the cues, prompts, and meaning of the patterns for the young adult to think and problem solve. In order for a young adult to be independent, he must be able to think and therefore express the language of his mental pictures in a way that is socially acceptable in a given community/society.

Therefore, if educators and parents want students to become independent, the students must learn to think in ways that allow a shared upon use of language. If students are not able to function independently, they may have learned to produce patterns for oral reading, for filling in worksheets, for writing sentences borrowed from books they read, for saying social rules, and so on, but not be able to understand the concepts. Sometimes students with ASD excel in a particular area of the curriculum, such as in art or science, but until they are asked to show their understanding with drawing and writing to represent the Language of Pictures, similar to how the physical science teacher asked students to draw a water shed, the refinement of the concepts may not happen. Patterns are easy to imitate, copy, or practice, but they do not always form concepts that are required for thinking and conceptually learning. An environment that is rich with literacy (e.g., Twatchman, 1992) helps build language and therefore thinking.

Figure 7.21 shows writing and drawing designed to help a student to learn the social choices related to the concept of upset. "Feeling upset" is a formal concept, just like electromagnetic waves, water shed, and where plants come from. *Formal concepts cannot be seen or touched without the Language of Pictures – without concepts being attached to the words.*

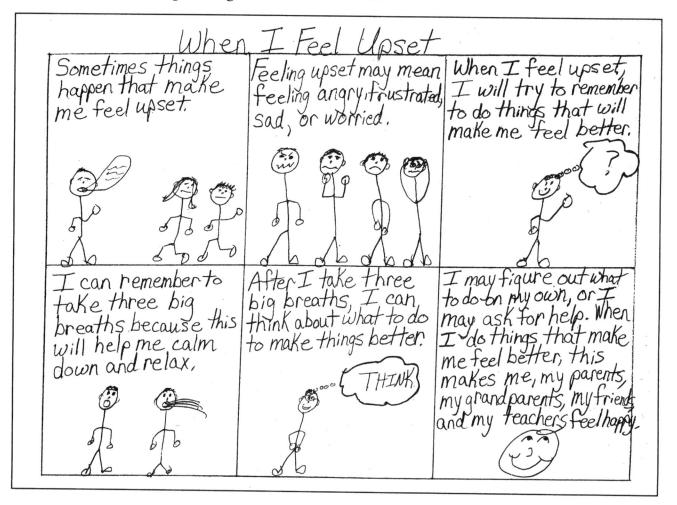

Figure 7.21. **When I feel upset.**

This contribution is printed with permission from Brenda Hiegel of Longview, Washington.

Activity: Why are most social concepts formal in nature?

Words must create pictures. Therefore, words need conceptual refinement. To help achieve that, the teacher or clinician draws the meaning of the student's written words. The student matches what he writes as motor patterns to the clinician's drawings of concepts that go with the writing. The student then rewrites the meaning, and this process goes back and forth until the student *truly has* the Language of Pictures for the concepts. This means that the student is learning not just the patterns but the concepts of the curriculum. Remember: Thinking necessitates the learning of concepts. Concepts underlie the development of language. Language represents the learner's development of concepts.

Since learning is socio-cognitive, the student's refinement of the cognitive learning also increases his social understanding of how meanings interrelate. By acquiring more formal types of meanings, the student develops increased language to become more independent. In this way, the writing and drawing affects the social concepts as well. Figure 7.22 shows another example of a social concept being refined through drawing and writing.

Figure 7.22. The student learns about the concept of interrupting.

This contribution is printed with permission from Brenda Hiegel of Longview, Washington.

Concepts are layers of meaning from multiple experiences of refinement, or of additional meaning being added. So the same student who learned about "feeling upset" and "not interrupting" must also learn about "listening." Figure 7.23 shows the same student learning about listening.

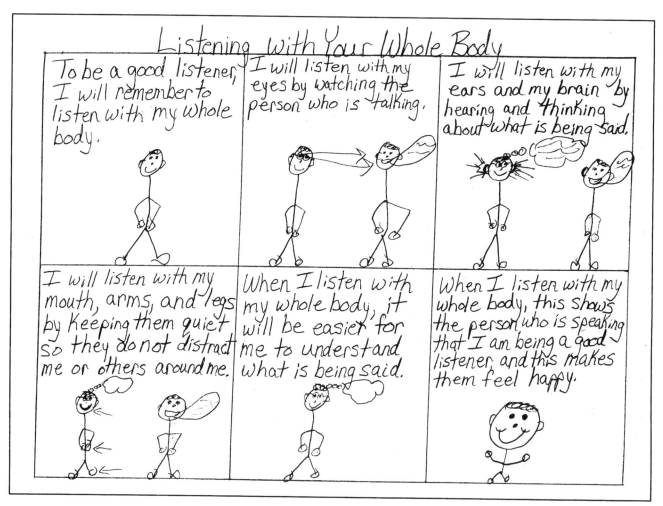

Figure 7.23. **Student learns about listening.**

This contribution is printed with permission from Brenda Hiegel of Longview, Washington.

Just like neurotypical students learn these socio-cognitive ideas from multiple spoken examples that overlap meaning, students with ASD learn these concepts through multiple overlapping motor movements of the pencil on the paper – writing to drawing, drawing to writing, and then more writing and drawing or drawing and writing.

This process of matching the concepts of the curriculum to what the student visually knows helps the student develop both social and cognitive concepts. For example, a student diagnosed with autism who needed social development also lacked cognitive understanding. In the example shown in Figure 7.24, the student and the classroom teacher work on the concepts related to different planets. The ideas are drawn and written about, but the conceptualization does not show interconnections of meaning. This suggests that the student in drawing and writing patterns, not concepts.

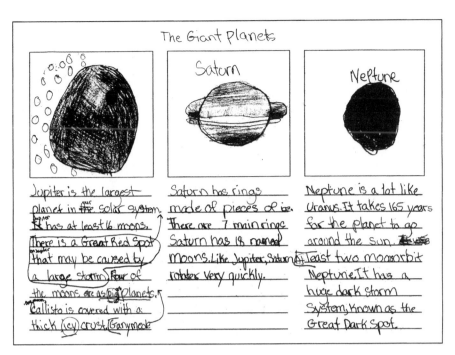

Figure 7.24. **Learning about concepts.**

Consequently, the concepts were drawn and written about as shown in Figure 7.25. The student was put into her picture as a person looking at the rings around Saturn. Then she was shown how people like her, called astronomers, look into the skies to see the various characteristics of planets.

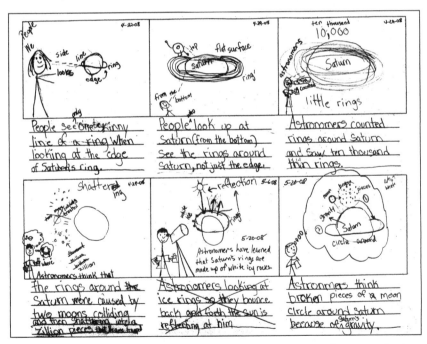

Figure 7.25. **The student learns about the meaning of the characteristics of planets through drawing and writing.**

Because this student learns best from motor movements of the hand to create visual concepts, the adult drew the pictures and the student wrote the language of the pictures. The teacher then wrote out the difference between writing patterns of words and understanding the drawings as concepts, as shown in Figure 7.26.

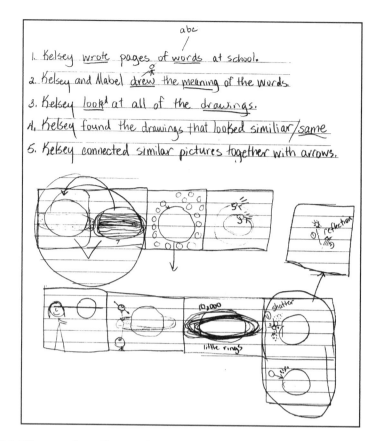

Figure 7.26. **The student learns how to connect written language to pictures.**

Activity: Why do content concepts and social concepts relate to each other?

Summary

Achieving within the curriculum requires more than just producing the patterns or skills of what the teacher offers. Learning the concepts underlying the curriculum requires both social and cognitive development within the student's neurobiological language learning system. Since individuals with ASD think using visual metacognition, the traditional academic patterns must be turned into concepts that can be drawn in real time and in a series of developmentally more advanced concepts. Students with ASD may not draw the concepts but can usually learn to use the print of language to explain what they understand of what the teacher draws.

As the teacher draws more ideas and helps the student match his written ideas to the drawn pictures, the student begins to think using more conceptualizations. Higher conceptualization results in more independent functioning. For example, to socially understand that there are many different groups of elected or appointed individuals making up "government," a person must understand all of the underlying "pictures" that define who these people are, what these people do, where these people work, what they do in their work, when they work, why they work, and how they work. When a person is able to understand all of the relationships among these concepts of government, then the person has a formal way of thinking about "government." This process of matching concepts with the written patterns creates the Language of Pictures for individuals with ASD.

CHAPTER 8
Making Visuals Easier

I see the picture now that you are there ...
I know what I see now that I have the words.
Your ideas make my pictures come to life!

Today's schools often invest in materials, methods, and curriculum packages designed to make the educator's job easier. Selection of such materials, methods, and curricula emphasizes the use of "research-based," effective practices. In this way, schools can prove that they are using "scientific, research-based" practices (Turnbull, Turnbull, & Wehmeyer, 2007), an important element in current educational legislation.

Although this is an admirable goal, such selections do not always work. For many decades, "good" teachers or support specialists have realized that when a practice, program, material, or curriculum did not work, the "obvious" response was to change what the teacher was doing. This type of thinking has recently acquired the name "response to intervention" or RTI (Turnbull et al., 2007). The thinking here is that the lack of effectiveness is a direct result of the "wrong" materials, methods, and/or curricula. However, most materials, methods, and/or curricula are useful and right for some child or group of children. The real issue is whether or not the methods, materials, and/or curricula are right for the child or children with which they are being used.

The previous chapters presented guideposts for use of drawing and pictures. The following list is designed to guide the thinking of educators and parents in deciding on materials, methods, and curricula to develop better interventions:

1. Effective interventions are as good as the developmental match between materials, such as visuals, and the child's level of cognitive, language, and social development.

2. Intervention is a process, not a product; so the more the educator or parent creates the meaning of the materials, like visuals, while working with the child, the more effective the process becomes.

3. Visuals have developmental levels as do all methods, materials, and curriculum packages.

4. Visuals are not just pictures but shapes that form from the movement of hands, lips, pencils, etc.

5. The use of language that is visual in nature is critical to students who learn visual concepts.

6. Materials, methods, and curricula must match the way the student learns.

Since most general education students learn in an auditory world (Arwood & Kaulitz, 2007), and since all individuals diagnosed with an autism spectrum disorder (ASD) learn with a visual brain, educators must ensure that materials, methods, and curricula focus on the visual way of thinking and learning so these students can succeed.

Since the English language and those who speak English use an auditory linguistic culture for teaching, it is important to translate the English sound of ideas into the visual graphics of concepts for individuals with ASD who are visual learners. The term coined by Arwood to refer to imposing properties of "visual languages" such as ASL (American Sign Language) and Mandarin Chinese onto an auditory language like English is Viconic language™ (Arwood & Brown, 2002). This chapter will discuss how to turn a spoken auditory English concept into something more visual through Viconic language™ methods.

Principles of Viconic Language™

English is a sound-based language (see Chapters 1 and 2), but individuals with ASD do not do well in processing sound into concepts (see Chapter 1 to 3). They can often imitate the patterns of sound very well, and they can often even translate mental visual thinking back into the patterns of sound (Arwood & Kaulitz, 2007). However, to learn visual concepts a person diagnosed with an ASD requires a visual process of using the movement of the shape of the mouth, the shape of the hands for signing, the shape of the movement of the pencil on the page, the shape of the strike of an old-fashioned typewriter, the shape of the hands word processing a word, and so forth. Individuals with ASD use these movements to create visual concepts resulting in a specific, non-auditory, visual way of thinking (Arwood & Brown, 2002).

The recognition that English must be switched into visual concepts, not just visual modes of input (see Preface), requires an understanding of how to translate the English language into visual concepts, like those typically found in languages like ASL and Mandarin Chinese. The characteristics of these visual languages (Arwood, 1991) include the use of context, principles of photographic and phonographic abilities, developmental hierarchy of graphics or visuals, and spatial properties.[9] Arwood uses the term "Viconic language™" to refer to the process of imposing these visual properties found in specific languages onto a sound-based culture that uses an auditory language like English. In other words, when the visual properties of visual types of languages are put onto the structure of an auditory language like English, the English sentence structures do not "sound" like English.

---

[9] Context creates meaning about the words before words are used. For example, in a visual culture a person would greet another person and talk about families before they would talk about business. Visual languages like American Sign Language or Mandarin Chinese are not alphabetic like English but use characters or signs to represent the pictures (mental photographs or graphics) of ideas. Even when sound (phonographic) is attached to these mental pictures, they refer to the meaning of ideas, not words. For example, in Chinese there are four different tones for the sounds "ma," which means four different ideas. But in English, an auditory language, different tones in saying a word does not change the meaning. Likewise, English is a time-based language that uses a lot of different ways to signal time (e.g., tenses, adverbs, specific time words like "after" or entire phrases "in the morning"). Visual languages, on the other hand, talk about how an event occurs in relationship to another event or the space (spatial) of an event. For example, when the sun comes up, we will go to market and sell our goods. The seller goes home when the goods are all sold or the sun goes down. Selling goods is an event accomplished in relationship to the context or space of the speaker, not based on time.

An example of an auditory phrase might be a parent telling a child "calm down." The child with ASD can learn to respond to this auditory phrase. That is, when the parent says, "Calm down," the child changes his behavior to appear to understand these words. In actuality, the child is responding to what she sees and hears in the context but not necessarily the meaning of the sound of the words.

So how does the child learn the conceptual meaning of the spoken words, "Calm down"? When the parent says, "Calm down!" these words are out of context (characteristic of auditory language). The words imply that the parent expects changes in the behavior *now* (time based), and the parents expect that the child can internalize the use of sound so that when the child complies, they figure it means that she understands why they want her to calm down.

Now impose the characteristics of a visual language like ASL (Arwood, 1991) onto the English phrase "Calm down." That is, add context, *make* ideas connect (context and spatial property), make ideas form a visual graphic. This is what the resulting Viconic language™ sounds like: "Jason, I see your arms move, your feet move. I see your face with a frown and I see tears on your face. When your arms move, feet move, and face has tears, then I cannot see what you see. So that I can see what you see and so I can see what to do to help you, I need to see your arms by your sides, your feet on the floor and your face with a mouth that is ready to talk. Then I can see what I need to do to help you."

To complete the visual graphic portion, the teacher drew Figure 8.1 while she was saying this Viconic language™.

Figure 8.1. **Child learns what to look like.**

The support personnel recorded an immediate change in the child's behavior as a result of using Viconic language™ (Lenius, 2007). The first-grade child stopped the tantrum. And because this teacher often changed her auditory English into Viconic language™, this student and others like him were able to be successful in her general education classroom.

The characteristics of visual languages can be imposed on any auditory material, method, and curriculum package, thereby increasing the effectiveness of the material, method, or curriculum package for children with ASD.

Activity: Why does imposing the characteristics of a visual language onto auditory language structures help children diagnosed with ASD?

Application of Viconic Language™

This section of the chapter will apply the principles of Viconic language™ to different visuals typically used with children diagnosed with ASD. Since most adults assume that a single picture or a picture of a symbol to represent an idea is the easiest type of visual, the first example focuses on "when" to use a single object picture as a symbol (Figure 8.2).

Figure 8.2. "Make."

Developmentally, this picture is not the easiest for a child with limited language (see Chapters 2 to 4) because the picture symbolizes different meanings of the concept "make." What shall we make? Who does the making? One could "make" a cake, "make" a joke, or "make" a disaster. The word "make" has many meanings determined by the context of the ideas. But pictures that symbolize concepts are effective when the learner is provided with sufficient context, and when the learner possesses the necessary language to connect the symbol with the intended meaning.

This symbol ("make") can be put into the context of a sentence, "What makes a good President?" (see Figure 8.3). The assumption is that the sentence helps a person understand the meaning of the word "make." The sentence gives the learner an understanding of the meaning for which "make" is being used, but the sentence structure does not add meaning to the concept. The conceptual meanings underlying the words add information; the way the words appear in a sentence does not add meaning.

A middle-school teacher who works with students with special needs successfully uses these types of symbolic visuals from News-2-You (Clark, 1997-2008; Mayer-Johnson, Symbolstix, 1981-2001; see Figure 8.3) to help her students *read* the meaning of the written words. But as we have seen earlier, reading the sentence does not mean the students have the understanding of the words of the sentence.

Figure 8.3. Think Page.

This teacher has noticed that most of her students want to answer this question with a personal belief, usually related to what they like or a copied pattern from a book or from what she said or wrote on the board. For example, a preoperational personal belief might result in the answer, "A good president likes ice cream." An imitated pattern from a textbook, might be "A good president is a strong leader." But this teacher wants more than personal beliefs that have little to do with an educated answer to the question, and she also wants more than imitated patterns. She wants the students to answer these types of questions with their own mental Language of Pictures so that what they write reflects what they know.

The answer to the question "What do you think makes a good president?" at a higher than preoperational belief level is really about what does a U.S. president (inferred type of president) do, when, where, how, and why? The questions that underlie the meaning of the first question imply that the duties of a U.S. president require some type of qualifications that support what the president does with whom, when, and where. This is a concrete level of understanding. The question could be answered concretely, "The president of the U.S. has to be able to fulfill a number of roles such as select a cabinet, sign bills submitted by Congress, and oversee the soldiers." This answer is concrete because the student provides examples of the roles that the president has to do.

The question could also be answered formally, "The president of the United States must be able to perform specific duties, including executive functions such as utilizing the power of a veto when appropriate, acting as head of state with other nations, being a responsible Commander of Chief for the military, and a figure head for the U.S. government and its people." This is a formal answer because the student is able to categorize the many different roles that a president is required to perform using the student's own wording based on the student's mental Language of Pictures.

Activity: What is a preoperational answer like? What is a concrete answer like? What is a formal answer like?

The higher the teacher's expectation for students' answers, the greater the need for students to learn from appropriate levels of visuals. Remember we started with a single word like "make" and its visual symbol, and already there is a lot of underlying language to consider. Also, keep in mind that in many schools, a copied answer from the board, from what the teacher said, or from the textbook is a correct answer – even though this type of imitation, copying, regurgitation, and/or replication is a simple pattern response that says nothing about the learner's level of conceptualization or understanding of the concepts. Nevertheless, the teacher in our example wants the students to *learn* the concepts, not just give patterns or belief statements.

Activity: What is the difference between answers that are pattern based and answers that are conceptually based?

Since our middle-school teacher wants her students to give more than a simple answer to the question "What do you think 'makes' a good president?" she must provide a series of layers of visuals from the easiest, or preoperational, level of meaning to a concrete level of meaning to a formal level of meaning, as these students are middle-school age. The teacher provides the language by following the characteristics of Viconic language™ as follows:

1. Add context. To add context, at least one person has to be put into the picture. The picture of "makes" in Figure 8.2 already has a person in it, so all it takes is to name the person and/or add language to connect that person to the child. The student must be in the picture to begin the process of learning a formal concept. This helps understand "make," but not the whole question.

2. Make the context spatial, which relates every idea to other ideas. In this way the visuals interconnect to form more complex meanings. "Visual" ideas relate and, therefore, must be connected. The more interconnections exist among the underlying concepts, the more visuals the teacher must provide so students can learn the language of the symbols.

3. Reduce the difficulty of a symbol like "make" by creating overlapping visuals of the topic. In a cartoon, the child is in her own picture, and the picture of child relates to the topic in every picture.

4. Use the same picture in the same event in multiple ways so the child develops the meaning of concepts such as "make" through the overlapping patterns of usage.

Activity: Why are the methods of Viconic language™ used to help children and adults with ASD learn concepts?

In applying the characteristics of Viconic language™, our middle-school teacher organizes the visuals around the topic of learning about the president of the United States in the following order. (Note: All of her students can read the sentence. The meaning underlying the sentence is what the students need to learn.)

1. *Make context.* First, the teacher provides context for the students so that they can see themselves in a picture of what they know about themselves. She draws, in real time, a student who represents any of the students in the classroom. In this drawing she provides information about him living at his home, in his town, in his state in the United States (see Figure 8.4).

Figure 8.4. **The student learns about his relationship to others.**

The teacher's oral language provides the meaning to what she draws. The Language of Pictures sounds something like this: This student, Charlie, lives with his mom, his parent. Mom manages the household. She works to earn money, pays bills, and so on. (The teacher also elicits ideas from the students.) Like Charlie, we all live in homes where someone manages the daily tasks of the home (again, the teacher asks the students to draw and write who is in each student's home and what the person who is in charge does). And all of our homes are in our town, Aurora. But there are other people nearby who live in other towns, like Hubbard. There are a lot of nearby towns, and all of these towns plus some big towns or cities are a part of the state we live in (this too is drawn).

2. *Make the context spatial.* To make this cognitively as relational as possible, the teacher talks with the students as she draws, about the specific town, specific state, and so on. And at each level there is someone managing the daily tasks – the parent, the mayor, the governor, the president. She also helps the students draw and/or write about each of these levels and who manages what. Notice that the drawing in Figure 8.4 shows these various concepts. By providing this type of context, the teacher assists the students in *relating* the meaning of what the students know to the new information that they will study. In this way, the teacher provides context, a Viconic language™ method. Remember this is a process: ***The drawing and talking, then drawing and writing again for more meaning, and then talking and drawing for additional meaning requires layers of visuals that may take several lessons.***

Activity: Why does the teacher draw the students into what they know before talking about the president?

3. *Create overlapping visuals.* Providing the student with context by putting the student into his own picture of who he lives with creates a preoperational introduction to the topic about the U.S. president. Beginning the lesson at a preoperational level is important because the learner is in his own picture. (The teacher may have to draw a boy and a girl thinking in order for more of the students to identify with the student the teacher drew. For some students with ASD, it is necessary to label the person with the student's name.) After the teacher and the students talk about how they connect to the topic, the teacher asks the students to draw and write about what they know about the president, the person managing the country. Figures 8.5a and 8.5b show the teacher drawing out a cartoon of what one student tells the class he knows about presidents.

Figure 8.5a. **One student knows that there are presidents' faces on money.**

This cartoon is a concrete layer of meaning added to the preoperational levels already drawn and talked about with the students. The students have their own cartoons and lined paper for taking notes and drawing their concepts of what the teacher talks about with them. Each student's knowledge is still preoperational, unless he or she can combine knowledge from multiple sources to create a concrete level of meaning. So the teacher shows the students how to obtain more information by cartooning out how to look in books for ideas (see Figure 8.5b). She continues with the information that one student offers – he knows about George Washington, so he will search the books for information about George Washington and draw and write about what he finds about George Washington. Figure 8.5b shows the process that all students will use. This collection of meaningful material provides the basis for a concrete understanding of what a president does.

Figure 8.5b. **The students will look in books for information about a president or about presidents.**

While the students research in the books, the teacher asks them to write the words that go with what they find in the books and/or draw[10] about what the words mean. In this way, each student has a personal connection to at least one president and a connection to what that one president did. This is a preoperational to concrete connection.

To move the students' learning from the preoperational knowledge level of what each knows to a concrete level of the rules about specific presidents or all presidents, the teacher asks the students to contribute what each has found in his/her book. As the students offer their knowledge, the teacher writes what they say and sometimes puts a picture on the board next to what they say. Then the teacher organizes the various pieces of research into categories of jobs and tasks, with the help of the students. By all students contributing what they drew and/or wrote about, their knowledge of what presidents do multiples. Multiple overlapping sets of visuals (preoperational to concrete) help develop knowledge at a higher concrete to formal level.

Activity: What is generally needed to move a student's conceptual learning from a preoperational to a concrete level of meaning?

4. *Use the same picture in the same event in multiple ways.* From the many layers of information that the teacher organized from the students' research about presidents, she draws the jobs of the president (see Figure 8.6), working off the students' listed, previously discussed contributions. She draws out what the students know into a flowchart. In Figure 8.6, there are four distinct bubble, each consisting of several lessons. The teacher uses the students' information to make the content for each bubble while making sure the content of what she draws is semantically accurate. For example, she looks up the content of the role of the U.S. president and then makes sure that she draws the correct meaning of that role.

---

[10] Some students will draw, some will write, and some will do both. Most students with ASD prefer to write patterns for which the teacher will have to help them draw concepts that will have more meaning than simply copying the written patterns from what they have seen in the books.

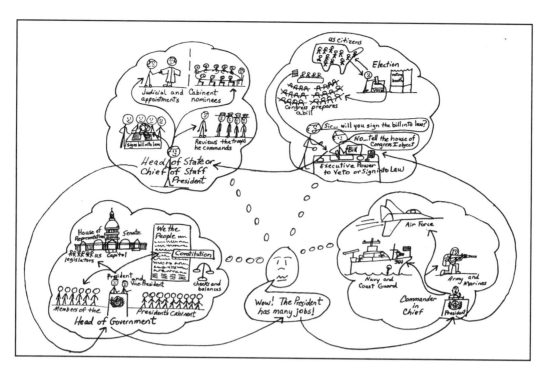

Figure 8.6. **Flowchart of the president's jobs.**

This set of tasks (students' contributions organized and then drawn and discussed) moves the students' knowledge from a concrete understanding to a more formal understanding when connected to an overall flowchart of what the president does. As she draws what the U.S. president does, the teacher checks orally with the students about what they know and connects what she draws back to the information they know. When students do not understand a set of concepts, she uses an arrow to pull out ideas that the students don't fully understand, such as what the president's cabinet consists of (see Figure 8.7), and draws those concepts in real time.

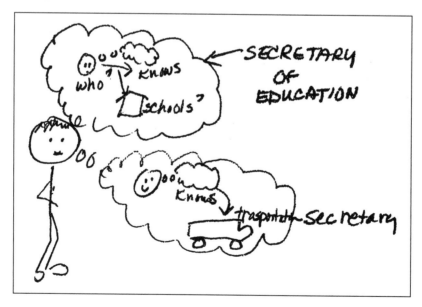

Figure 8.7. **The president selects his cabinet members.**
(The teacher drew out 15 thought bubbles for the 15 different cabinet members.)

It is the multiple bubbles in Figure 8.6, along with the explanations with cartooning (see Figures 8.5a and 8.5b) and the students' contributions, that help develop the concrete level of the concept of what a U.S. president does. After the students have developed sufficient knowledge by receiving the appropriate levels of visuals through Viconic language™ methods, they are ready to use a Think Page (News-2-You, 1997-2008) with Symbolstix (see Figure 8.3). The students have sufficient language to use the symbols to read as well as understand a more concrete, formal level of meaning of the question. When the students understand the question at a higher conceptual level, they are better able to answer the question at a higher conceptual level. At this point, "makes" has multiple underlying visuals when it is in the context of the president's jobs.

> ### Activity: Why does it help a child to learn a concept by arranging visuals in a developmental order from the preoperational level, through multiple concrete examples, to the formal level?

Did the teacher make good use of the knowledge about Viconic language™? Did she use the characteristics of Viconic language™ in developing the students' understanding of what a U.S. president does and, therefore, what makes a good president.

The answer is yes. First of all, the teacher used a lot of context. By beginning in their own homes, the students became agents, engaging in actions with their parents, in their homes. Second, the teacher connected this context to all of their homes being in a town. This allowed for a spatial connection or relationship between each student and the other students in the classroom. Third, she arranged the order of presentation from what is easiest cognitively to what is most difficult – from preoperational to concrete to formal – using the pure symbols for a formal concept (president) last. Finally, she made sure that the concept of what the president does and, therefore, what makes a good president, was used in multiple ways (flowchart) so that the students had an opportunity to overlap the concrete examples of what a president does into the formal concept of what makes a good president. In this way, the students acquired their Language of Pictures about very formal concepts.

> ### Activity: What are some ways in which a symbol can be simplified by using the characteristics of Viconic language™?

A second example of how to apply the methods of Viconic language™ involves Charlotte. Charlotte was a nonverbal, aggressive teen diagnosed with autism, who began the process of learning symbols through H/H activities that were drawn out with her in the picture. Eventually, she developed enough of the overlapping concepts to be able to create context. The adults could then do a quick symbolic sketch with the written words, and Charlotte was able to follow the words with the pictures. Figure 8.8 shows Charlotte's Friday.

Figure 8.8. **Charlotte does her Friday.**

Because Charlotte is in her own picture as an agent and "walking" through the Language of Pictures of what the day looks like, the task is preoperational to her and the pictures of the car, though symbolic, will work for her. These pictures of Charlotte's Friday includes context, multiple relationships of Charlotte to her day, and the symbols are simplified by being related to her.

Activity: Why does the picture of what Charlotte does on Friday work for her?

Any time a visual represents more than what can be seen with the eye, it becomes more difficult because the person looking at it has to bring his or her language to the situation to complete the missing parts to form a complete picture. For example, individuals with ASD often have difficulty reading between the lines, such as reading what a face means. In Figure 8.9 Lyn Larfield, a speech-language pathologist in Vancouver, Washington, drew out with written language what faces tell the student (used with permission).

What do people's faces tell me?

When I hear things that people say, sometimes their faces do not match their words. I need to make sure I look at people's faces to see if the words match the way their face looks, because if the people's words match their face it means one thing and if the people's words don't match their fact it means something different. When I look at people's faces to figure out what they mean, it's called reading their facial expressions.

If I hear words that make me think that the person is mad at me and I see a face that looks mad, the person is probably mad at me. I can ask the person why they are mad.

If I hear words that sound mad, but I see a face that is smiling, the person probably is making a joke or is teasing me. I can laugh with them. If I'm not sure if the person is joking, I can ask them.

If I hear words that sound silly, but the person has a mad face, the person probably is joking with me. I can laugh or ask them if they are joking if I'm not sure.

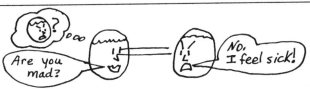

Sometimes when I look at people's faces its hard to tell what they are feeling. When a person is tired or sick, sometimes they look like they have a mad face. I can check to see if the person is mad by asking them if they are mad.

Figure 8.9. **What faces tell me.**

The written language Lyn uses in Figure 8.9 overlaps and creates verbal context for the concepts. However, some students need to be able to see the concepts that the written language represent, and these drawings of floating heads would be too difficult for them because they would have to bring too much language to the picture. That is, the learner looking at the pictures would have to make language connections that would sound something like this: "I see eyes, hair, and so on, that look like those of a person so this must be the head of a person." Actually, this language is fairly brief for what is really missing, because the person looking at the parts of a head must be able to recognize that these are parts of a whole (psychological clozure) concept. The drawing is symbolized at a formal level[11] while the language

---

[11] A formal level of language means that the ideas require multiple pictures to be understood; that is, one cannot see, touch, or feel a formal concept. Floating heads are formal because they are never really seen.

is written at more of a preoperational level. To connect the preoperational written language to what the language conceptually represents, apply the Viconic language™ characteristics:

1. Add context. Draw the stick figure part of the rest of the person. Put the person into the picture (see Figure 8.10).

What do people's faces tell me?

When I hear things that people say, sometimes their faces do not match their words. I need to make sure I look at people's faces to see if the words match the way their face looks, because if the people's words match their face it means one thing and if the people's words don't match their fact it means something different. When I look at people's faces to figure out what they mean, it's called reading their facial expressions.

If I hear words that make me think that the person is mad at me and I see a face that looks mad, the person is probably mad at me. I can ask the person why they are mad.

If I hear words that sound mad, but I see a face that is smiling, the person probably is making a joke or is teasing me. I can laugh with them. If I'm not sure if the person is joking, I can ask them.

If I hear words that sound silly, but the person has a mad face, the person probably is joking with me. I can laugh or ask them if they are joking if I'm not sure.

Sometimes when I look at people's faces its hard to tell what they are feeling. When a person is tired or sick, sometimes they look like they have a mad face. I can check to see if the person is mad by asking them if they are mad.

2. Now put the words to the picture so that the child can see what the picture means. Notice the explanation of the "garbage man" in the third set of pictures (see Figure 8.10). This specific example helps the student relate to the meaning of the pictures and words.

3. Note that a lot of the written language in Figure 8.10 does not sound like typical English (it has the relational properties of a visual language). The ideas overlap or relate. "When I hear things that people say, sometimes their faces do not match their words. I need to make sure I look at people's faces to see of the words match the way their face looks ..." The words continue to overlap to make connections.

4. Adding more words, drawing the whole person, and grounding the person makes the task easier. This task could become even easier by making it specific to one child and to specific examples of what the child hears, sees, etc. In this way, generic terms like "people" would be replaced with a specific name, like Brad, or specific referent such as "boy."

By using the characteristics of Viconic language™ with the pictures about faces, Lyn is able to adjust the difficulty level of this lesson for different students with different language, cognitive, and social developmental needs. In this way, the Language of Pictures occurs at the child's level of learning.

> ### *Activity: Why is it important for learning to include the context of a person in pictures of concepts?*

The next example of the Language of Pictures is about something easier than learning what "makes" a good U.S. president or how we interpret people's faces. This example is from an elementary-age child who often struggles with relationships between himself and others. The child's father drew the cartoon in Figure 8.11. Notice that once the dad drew the child, Owen, into his picture, Dad could draw the heads with muffs but without bodies and Owen still understood that the heads were symbolic for him, his brother Cooper, and his dad. The cartoon was very effective. Owen knew what to do, what to look like, and how to behave.

Figure 8.11. **Daddy takes Owen to the races.**

The next cartoon helps Owen understand that there are consequences to his behavior. If Owen cannot play with his brother properly, the toys may be taken away from both children. Besides, Cooper receives Dad's attention because he hurts from Owen hitting him. Again, the cartoon works because it is drawn in real time when Owen needs to be able to see how his actions affect others. When Owen cannot play with his brother, that choice also affects Owen's ability to play with the toys (see Figure 8.12).

Figure 8.12. **Owen learns that hitting his brother has consequences.**

Owen needs lots of information about how to ask, tell, or command others to do tasks. As illustrated in Figures 8.11 and 8.12, Owen needs to see others in his picture. From Owen's perspective, he is there at the pleasure of what others can do for him. He is functioning at a preoperational level of social development – he is an agent, and the world revolves around him. So Owen drops a toy car and says, "I dropped my car." Owen becomes agitated and repeats the phrase over and over and over. Dad hears him and responds, "Yep, you dropped your car" (see Figure 8.13).

Figure 8.13. **Owen drops his car.**

Owen telling his dad that he dropped his car does not explain what he wants. Owen wants his car. So he says, "Give me my car!" which affects how Dad sees Owen. Mabel, Owen's teacher, draws out the various ways in which Owen can use language (see discussion of performatives in Chapter 7) in this situation. Owen has adequate language but does not know how to use it to get others to understand his needs. Multiple individual pictures in Figure 8.13 show Owen the various ways he can talk about the dropped car with his dad. In this way, how Owen uses language affects how Dad perceives the situation. ***Different language results in different pictures. Different pictures indicate what the language means.***

> ## *Activity: How does language change the meaning of pictures? How does the Language of Pictures develop from pictures, or what a person sees?*

The more advanced the concept is, the greater the language level must be. Pictures are the concepts, so when a child needs to understand more complex concepts, the parent or teacher must use more pictures. Owen sitting with his dad and watching the car races was a simple concept for Owen because he had the language. He just needed the pictures or concepts to go with the words. When Dad drew the concepts and wrote the words, Owen could see what Dad meant when he told him how to behave at the car races. In this way, Dad's drawing provided Owen with the Language of Pictures about how to behave when going to a car race.

But concepts like friendship are more difficult. They are formal and need a lot of visuals. Figure 8.14 shows a lot of drawing for another child, Sam. Sam's behavior (e.g., punching) affects other students, who then do not want to be friendly or act like a friend to Sam.

Figure 8.14. **Multiple cartoons about being a friend.**

Notice that the cartoon starts with specific incidents related to Sam and other students. This is followed by pictures of "friend types" of behaviors that would replace the slamming of the door, the punching, the holding, and the name calling. In this way, Sam can choose to listen, use words, and/or walk away. Finally, on the right side of the paper, Sam is given some visual ways to decide what matters in others' behavior and what doesn't matter. All three sets of ideas (what he does, what he could do, and whether or not what others do matters) are all pieces of what develops a formal understanding of "friendship."

These types of complex concepts cannot be learned (conceptually) using single pictures. Multiple sets of visuals that are interconnected and relate (Viconic language™) to one another must be used to create complex levels of meaning of concepts. ***Concepts are not learned in isolation. Therefore, visuals that provide the Language of Pictures must represent the complexity of the concepts by using multiple visuals that interconnect;*** otherwise, children (especially with ASD) repeat back patterns of what they see on a page or what others say without understanding the meaning of the printed or spoken words.

Even these three sets of pictures drawn in real time with specific, actual situations with Sam are not enough Language of Pictures for formal concepts. Figure 8.15 shows Sam writing out the words.

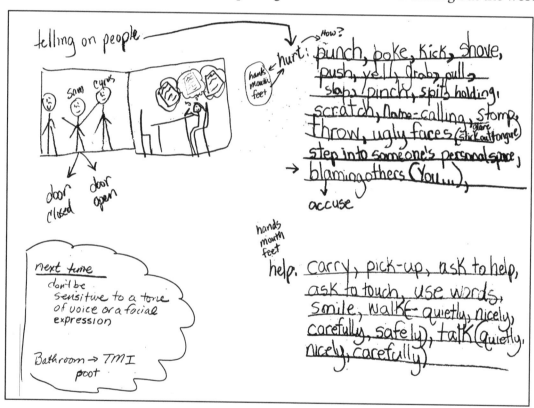

***Figure 8.15.* Sam is writing out the words to match language with the pictures.**

Sam's written words are the language patterns for the concepts that Mabel drew with him. When the language and the visuals go together, Sam is able to learn the Language of Pictures. He knows the meaning of the spoken words because the written (visual-motor) words connect the language to the concepts.

Sam is learning many of the formal concepts, such as how much time a behavior or event takes and how to treat his classmates with respect. These concepts also help him form the Language of Pictures about "friendship." Figure 8.16 shows another session of drawing. Mabel draws and Sam writes.

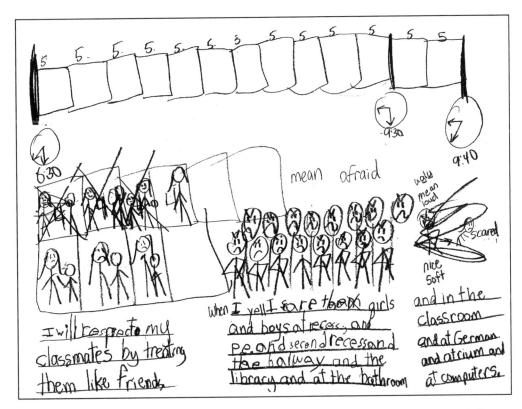

Figure 8.16. Sam learns how respect is part of the concept of friendship.

For Sam, different situations provide opportunities for him to learn more and more about friendship. Figure 8.17 shows Sam how the language of classroom rules fit with what he does with his body.

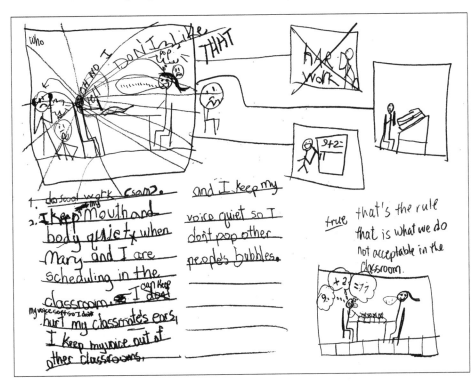

Figure 8.17. Sam learns how behavioral acts represent the rules as part of the concept of "friendship."

Making Visuals Easier

Lots and lots of drawings and writings are matched to develop a higher conceptual meaning of friendship. Until an individual can acquire enough conceptual meaning to understand rules, he or she cannot become independent. Independence for many individuals with ASD is a matter of learning the Language of Pictures of what formal concepts like "friendship" mean at a concrete level of understanding rules about the concepts. Understanding friendship as it relates only to the individual's needs is insufficient to live safely and independently. Friendship is about the relationship between and among people. If an individual only thinks about himself, he has little ability to think about how others' actions might affect him or how his actions might affect others. For example, if a person thinks only about himself, he might forget that the pan on the stove will catch fire and burn down his house because he cannot see how his actions affect other people or their objects. He might not lock the door because he might not realize that others could come into his home, and so forth. Concrete, rule-governed meaning of formal concepts like friendship requires multiple overlapping sets of pictures to create the Language of Pictures.

Activity: What level of language functioning for social and cognitive tasks must a person develop to truly become independent?

The next example of a Viconic language™ application begins with the educator and the student in a conversation about a Social Story™ (Gray, 1994, 2000)[12] on how to be a good sport when playing games. Figure 8.18 shows the story.

Figure 8.18. **A narrative about the social rules related to being a good sport when playing games, contributed by Lyn Larfield of Vancouver, Washington, and used with permission.**

---

[12]   The term "Social Stories™" is specific to a process discussed by Carol Gray (1994, 2000).

For many students on the autism spectrum who function at a high level of language development, this social narrative works much of the time for many specific instances. But if the child is struggling with developing concepts used within the Social Story™, more writing and drawing for the student is needed. Figures 8.19a and 8.19b show a drawing used to help debrief and calm a student after a "blow-out" in order to provide him with an action plan; a way to have enough Language of Pictures to understand what he does when he "plays games" with other students at recess.

Figures 8.19a and 8.19b. **This drawing is a preoperational to concrete visual to help a student to learn the concepts of how to play games with other students at recess. It has the student in the pictures (preoperational), but there are also rules (concrete) about playing with other students.**

Sometimes parents and educators think they are providing sufficient Language of Pictures when they present a rule with a symbolic drawing as shown in Figure 8.20. However, for most students who need visuals to learn concepts, this type of written and drawn rule does not provide enough context or relational information for concept development.

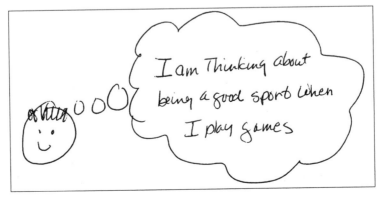

Figure 8.20. **A thought bubble about a rule.**

The easiest way to tell if the visuals provide enough information is to try them; if they work, then the student understands the Language of Pictures. If the student does not change her behavior or actions, the visual does not work, and the student needs more language about the pictures. If the visuals do not work, use some of the Viconic language™ methods to make the visuals provide more of the Language of Pictures. Figures 8.21 and 8.22 show a difference in developmental level of the pictures. In Figure 8.21 the teacher draws out, tells, and writes for John what "interrupt" means.

Figure 8.21. John "interrupts" and makes the teacher's and students' mental pictures vanish.

From Arwood, E., & Brown, M. (1999). *A guide to cartooning and flowcharting* (p. 2). Portland, OR: APRICOT, Inc.
Reprinted with permission.

The cartoon in Figure 8.21 is a preoperational visual of what the student does that is called "interrupting" and the resulting consequences or actions. Figure 8.22 is a concrete to formal example of what it means to "interrupt."

Figure 8.21 lowers the cognitive language level of the concept of interrupting to a preoperational level. Remember that by putting the child into the picture, we revert back to the preoperational level. Figure 8.22 offers a visual for the same concept of interrupting at a concrete (rule-governed), formal level (applied rules to general situations). Both examples work, depending on the level of the student's language and social cognition. Figure 8.21 works for students learning the concept of "interrupting." Figure 8.22 works better for students who know what "interrupt" means, but for whom the adult wants to provide rules or reminders.

Listening and Talking in a Small Group

There are a lot of times that I have to be a good listener. I listen to my teacher, my parents, and my friends. Sometimes, I am in a small group of three, four or five people and I have to listen and figure out when it's o'kay to talk.

In a group, only one person talks and the rest of the people listen and watch. While someone talks, I can watch to see what the person is saying and make pictures in my head about what that person is saying.

The pictures will make me want to talk, but I must wait until that person is finished talking before I start talking. If two people talk at the same time, no one can see what either person is saying because our words overlap. That is called interrupting.

Figure 8.22. **Listening and talking in a small group.**

Contributed by Lyn Larfied, Vancouver, Washington. Used with permission.

One application of Viconic language™ methods that has not been discussed in this book involves using the Language of Pictures to just help bring a student's level of language up; not for a specific topic, a specific concept, a specific setting, or even a specific rule for choice or behavior. When a parent or educator is very skilled at overlapping the patterns of language with the concepts of meaning, a child's language will increase, not just for the current lesson but for other lessons.

Figures 8.23-8.27 show a written discussion between Mabel and Jonathan about one aspect of cars. The purpose was to raise Jonathan's overall language level, not to teach about cars. He was learning about something that was of interest and was teenage-appropriate, as well as using language to raise his thinking level.

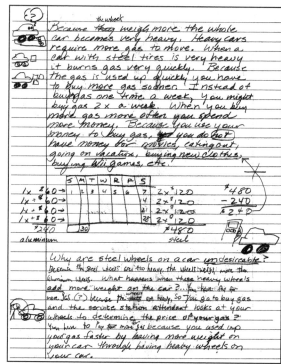

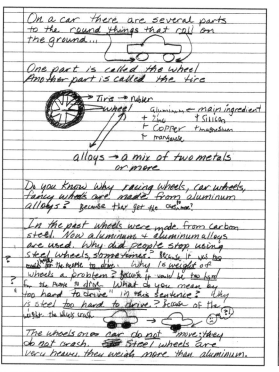

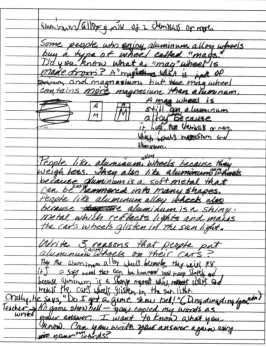

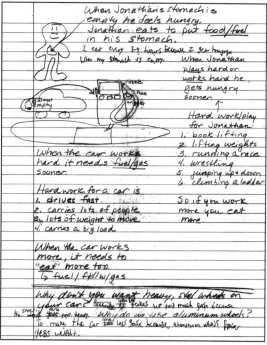

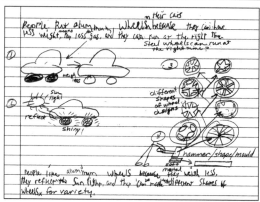

Figures 8.23-8.27. **A discussion in writing about car wheels.**

Jonathan learns concepts best when the written language patterns match the meaning of the visual words. In Figure 8.28, Mabel asks Jonathan to draw about the written words that they shared in Figures 8.23-8.27 in order to refine his conceptualization of the meaning of the language about the words.

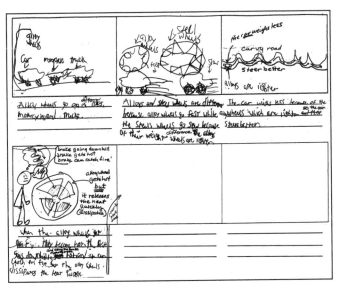

Figure 8.28. Jonathan draws his understanding of the written words.

Mabel continues to add language to represent Jonathan's concepts by writing more words to assign meaning to his concepts as shown in Figure 8.29.

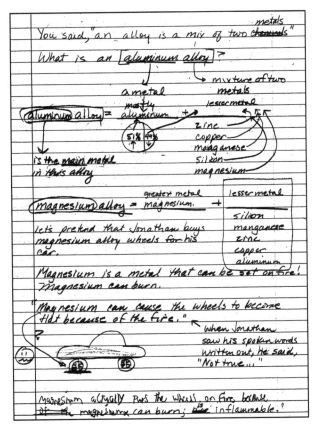

Figure 8.29. Jonathan and Mabel write about what Jonathan drew and wrote.

The purpose of working from visual patterns of print and writing to the concepts and back to the print is to scaffold[13] a motor or movement access to the pictures or visuals. Since most individuals with ASD learn best this way, connecting a visual form of language structure such as print in context with the drawn pictures allows for the best conceptualization.

All visuals have a language level and a socio-cognitive level that represents what a user of the visuals knows or understands. Even the task of giving grades is difficult to understand unless the teacher is able to provide an appropriate level of visuals to create the Language of Pictures. Figure 8.30 is part of a report card drawn with visuals to represent the levels of performance corresponding to levels of accomplishment.

Figure 8.30. **Report card.**

Contributed by Nicki Roggenkamp and Nikki Ekle, Vancouver, Washington. Used with permission.

---

[13] "Scaffolding" means to assign meaning to something another person does in response to meaning expressed from something the adult does. The child does something, and the educator assigns meaning with another movement or act. Then the child does another movement, and the adult assigns meaning again with more movement, similar movement, or different meaning.

All visuals contribute to the Language of Pictures. Even the rules for Viconic language™ strategies can be learned through pictures, drawings of concepts, and shapes, which are written words or patterns of language. Figure 8.31 is an example of a student who is learning how to learn through the Language of Pictures.

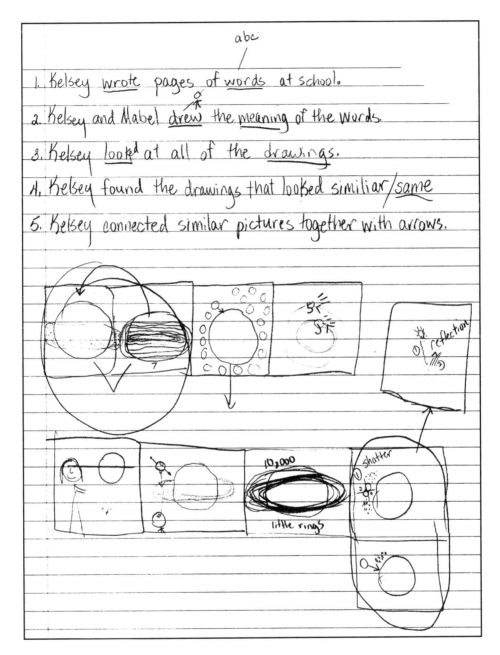

Figure 8.31. **Kelsey is learning to learn through the Language of Pictures.**

Activity: What are some applications of Viconic language™?

This chapter presented a variety of ways to impose visual language characteristics onto an auditory language like English to provide individuals with ASD the Language of Pictures. The characteristics of Viconic language™ include the following:

1. *Add context.* Context refers to people, agents, and actions that interrelate. To add context, at least one person has to be in a contextual picture. By putting a person into the picture, the basic agent, action, object relationships are utilized, which provides a preoperational level of visual, which is where all new concepts are learned. This begins the journey of acquiring the Language of Pictures.

2. *Make the context spatial.* "Visual" ideas relate and are connected. Visually depict the child in relationship to the picture and any objects and actions in the picture. Draw the concepts, write the language. Then write the language and draw new concepts, and so forth. This scaffolds the meaning of the visuals to create more Language of Pictures.

3. *Reduce the difficulty of symbols or language by creating overlapping visuals of the topic.* For example, a cartoon showing a child in a series of related pictures is easier to understand than a symbol that represents all the pictures in the cartoon. Acquiring the Language of Pictures is based on matching the child's developmental level to the visual and vice versa.

4. *Use the same visual in the same event in multiple ways.* In this way, the child develops the meaning of concepts through the overlapping patterns of usage. That is, the child is not just producing patterns but learning the Language of Pictures.

Summary

The Language of Pictures refers to how to use visual thinking strategies to help children and adults diagnosed with ASD learn to better conceptualize higher-order thinking, develop social competence, and learn solid academic skills. By aligning a child's thinking system with the way material is presented, a child can learn the Language of Pictures. Oral language as well as the language of pictures must be changed to match the way a child or adult learns to form concepts as a way to think. One way to change English, an auditory language, into a form that matches the thinking of a person with ASD is to impose the characteristics of a visual language onto the English. This process uses the Viconic language™ characteristics to guide the choice of "visuals" to help individuals think better conceptually.

We wish you every success in your application of Viconic language™ methods.

REFERENCES

Arwood, E. (1983). *Pragmaticism: Theory and application.* Rockville, MD: Aspen Systems Corporation.

Arwood, E. (1985). *APRICOT I MANUAL and 50 pictures.* Portland, OR: APRICOT Inc.

Arwood, E. (1989). *APRICOT II MANUAL.* Portland, OR: APRICOT, Inc.

Arwood, E. (1991). *Semantic and pragmatic language disorders* (2nd ed.). Rockville, MD: Aspen Systems Corporation.

Arwood, E., & Brown, M. (1999). *A guide to cartooning and flowcharting.* Portland, OR: APRICOT, Inc.

Arwood, E., & Brown, M. (2001). *A guide to visual strategies for young adults.* Portland, OR: APRICOT, Inc.

Arwood, E., & Brown, M. (2002). *Balanced literacy: Phonics, viconics, kinesics, aspect.* Portland, OR: APRICOT, Inc.

Arwood, E., & Brown, M. (2007, November). *A therapeutic protocol for visual language meaning.* Presentation: Language is Learning: The Metacognitive Basis to Symbolization and Semantic Memory, Portland, Oregon.

Arwood, E., Brown, M., & Robb, B. (2005). *Make it visual in the classroom: I'm in your picture.* Portland, OR: APRICOT, Inc.

Arwood, E., & Kaakinen, J. (2004, Winter). Visual language strategies for innovative teaching of science. *Journal of Science Education for Students with Disabilities, 10,* 27-36.

Arwood, E., & Kaulitz, C. (2007). *Learning with a visual brain in an auditory world: Visual language strategies for individuals with autism spectrum disorders.* Shawnee Mission, KS: Autism Asperger Publishing Company.

Arwood, E., & Robb, B. (2008). Language events in a classroom. *The ESL Magazine, 61,* 9-15.

Arwood, E., & Unruh, I. (2000). *Event-based learning handbook.* Portland, OR: APRICOT, Inc.

Arwood, E., & Young, E. (2000). *The language of respect: The Right of Each Student to Participate in an Environment of Communicative Thoughtfulness.* La Vergne, TN: Lightning Press. POD by APRICOT, Inc.

Bondy, A., & Frost, L. (2001) *A picture's worth: PECS and other visual communication strategies in autism.* Bethesda, MD: Woodbine House.

Buron, D. (2007). Social cognition: What is it and what does it tell us about how to teach? *Autism Advocate, 48,* 35-38.

Clark, J. *News-2-You,* Inc. (1997-2008). Huron, OH: Symbolstix, LLC.

Dunn, L., & Dunn, D. (2007). *Peabody Picture Vocabulary Test, Fourth Edition.* Minneapolis, MN: NCS Pearson, Inc.

Gately, S. E. (2008). Facilitating reading comprehension for students on the autism spectrum. *Teaching Exceptional Children, 40*(3), 40-45.

Grandin, T. (1992). An inside view of autism. In E. Schopler & G. Mesibov (Eds.), *High functioning individuals with autism* (pp. 116-123). New York: Platinum Press.

Grandin, T. (1995). *Thinking in pictures.* New York: Doubleday Publishers.

Grandin, T. (2005). *Animals in translation.* Orlando, FL: A Harvest Book, Harcourt.

Gray, C. (1994). *Comic strip conversations.* Arlington, TX: Future Horizons.

Gray, C. (2000). *The new social story book, illustrated edition.* Arlington, TX: Future Horizons.

Gray, C., & Garand, J. (1993). Social Stories™: Improving responses of students with autism with accurate social information. *Focus on Autistic Behavior, 8,* 1-10.

Jensen, E. (1998). *Teaching with the brain in mind.* Alexandria, VA: Association for Supervision and Curriculum Development.

Lenius, M. (2007). *The use of gentle teaching to reduce inappropriate classroom behavior.* Unpublished thesis, University of Portland, Portland, OR.

Logothetis, N. K. (2007). Vision: A window of consciousness. In F. E. Bloom (Ed.), *Best of the brain from Scientific American* (pp. 79-89). Washington, DC: The Dana Center.

Lucas, E. (1980). *Semantic and pragmatic language disorders: Assessment and remediation.* Rockville, MD: Aspen Systems Corporation.

Martinez-Conde, S., & Macknik, S. (2007). Windows on the mind. *Scientific American, 297*(2), 56-63.

Mayer-Johnson. (1981-2001). *The picture communication symbols ©1981-2008 by Mayer-Johnson LLC.* Boardmaker™ is a trademark of Mayer-Johnson LLC. San Diego, CA: Author.

Ramachandran, V. S., & Oberman, L. M. (2006). Broken mirrors. *Scientific American, 11,* 63-69.

Rizzolatti, G., Fogassi, L., & Gallese, V. (2006). Mirrors in the mind. *Scientific American, 11,* 54-61.

Skinner, B. F. (1974) *About behaviorism.* New York: Random House.

Slater, J. (1994-2006). *Picture it.* Guffey, CO: Slater Software, Inc.

Turnbull, A., Turnbull, R., & Wehmeyer, M. L. (2007). *Exceptional lives* (5th ed.). Upper Saddle River, NJ: Pearson.

Twatchman, D. (1992). *Sense making: Merging the wisdom of pragmatics with literacy-rich new ideas.* Presentation at annual conference of the Autism Society of America.

Walker, H. M., Ramsey, E., & Gresham, F. M. (2004). *Antisocial behavior in school* (2nd ed.). Belmont, CA: Wadsworth.

West, T. C. (1997). *In the mind's eye.* Amherst, NY: Prometheus Books.

Winner, M. G. (2000). *Inside out: What makes a person with social cognitive deficits tick?* San Jose, CA: Michelle Garcia Winner Publisher.

Winner, M. G. (2007). *A politically incorrect look at evidence-based practices and teaching social skills: A literature review and discussion.* San Jose, CA: Michelle Garcia Winner Publisher.

Winner, M. G. (2007). *Thinking about you, thinking about me* (2nd ed.). San Jose, CA: Michelle Garcia Winner Publisher.

GLOSSARY

Acoustic patterns – features of sound that can be copied, echoed, and/or imitated without conceptualization or understanding.

Agency/agent – someone who does something; part of a basic semantic relationship.

Antisocial behavior – on the negative end of a continuum of social competence; antisocial behavior does not contribute to the development of healthy relationships.

Arwood's Neurosemantic Language Learning Theory – a term coined by Ellyn Arwood, which states that learning is a socio-cognitive process of acquiring language through four meaningful stages: Sensory Input, Perceptual Pattern Development, Concept Development, and Language Development.

Auditory learning system – acoustic patterns integrated with visual patterns to form language-based auditory concepts.

Autism spectrum disorders (ASD) – a term that encompasses autism and similar disorders as listed in the DSM-IV (*Diagnostic and Statistical Manual of Mental Disorders-Fourth Edition*; American Psychiatric Association, 2004). Specifically, Asperger Syndrome, PDD-NOS, childhood disintegrative disorder, and Rett's Syndrome.

Behavior – a series of acts that are observable and countable.

Cognition – the physiological organization of sensation into the basic thought patterns, or how we think.

Cognitive relationship – a relationship made up of an agent, an action, and an object (i.e., who does what to whom or what).

Concepts – systems of perceptions or recognized patterns that interconnect to form new meanings (i.e., understanding ideas that have layers of meaning such as "sit," "work," "government," "respect").

Concrete level of cognitive development/thinking – characterized by the mastery of logic and rational thinking (i.e., agency is about one who relates to others, understands the concept of "we," and the meaning of rules, but not why the rules are in place. Preoperational thinking, on the other hand, is all about me … my bed, my clothes, my class, my school, my toys.

Context – the surrounding, related information of a concept that helps explain its meaning (i.e., the context refers to the who, what, where, when, how, and why of agents, actions, and their objects).

Conventions/conventional language – the mutually used tools of sign representation between a speaker and a listener. For example, most speakers of English share a similar meaning for the word "table."

Formal level of cognitive development/thinking – characterized by the development of abstract ideas that cannot be seen, touched, or heard; includes critical and hypothetical thinking as well as displaced problem solving and the ability to walk in the shoes of another speaker. Concepts such as responsible, considerate, justice, government, and respect are "formal."

Iconic – a sign (as a word or graphic symbol) whose form suggests its meaning.

Language – the way people communicate their thinking or thoughts to others in a recognizable or conventional manner and form; the tool of verbal communication. Language is the fourth stage of Arwood's Neurosemantic Language Learning Theory, where language represents concepts.

Language functions – processes of how language works to develop social and cognitive learning.

Learning styles – educational preferences for learning that may be the result of specific training. It may not be the same as the neurobiological learning system's way of learning new concepts.

Mirror neurons – the neurons responsible, in part, for the ability to see what others do and the ability to imitate their actions.

Motor patterns – recognizable forms of motor input (i.e., recognizing the movement of a person's feet as walking or the movement of the tongue in one's mouth to form an English word). Motor patterns create mental *shapes* of ideas.

Metacognition – the language used to think about thinking.

Neurobiological – the knowledge of how cells interact based on their biological nature.

Neurosemantic language learning – the physical process of learning the language of meaning through recognition of perceptual patterns from sensory input to form concepts; see Arwood's Neurosemantic Language Learning Theory.

Perception – the separation and organization of sensory input into recognizable patterns of meaning; the second stage of the Neurosemantic Language Learning Theory.

Perceptual patterns – the organization of sensory-received stimuli into usable features (i.e., sounds, tastes, touch, smells, and sights all integrate as sets of perceptual patterns that overlap into concepts).

Performative – a verb that performs an act when uttered, such as to promise, to lie, to invite, etc.

Preoperational stage of cognitive development/thinking – characterized by seeing the world only from the child's perspective and not in relationship to others (i.e., agency is about "me." I am the only person in the world. It's my chair, my toys, my friend).

Prosocial behavior – behavior that increases the likelihood of a child becoming socially competent, which means he or she is able to initiate and maintain healthy relationships. Prosocial behavior consists of acts that are acceptable by society for the purpose of furthering the development of others in society.

Semantic relationship – a set of concepts represented verbally or nonverbally; a basic semantic relationship consists of an agent, an action, and an object. Basic semantic relationships form the building block of language (i.e., mom throws ball).

Sensori-motor stage of development/thinking – characterized by the relationship between incoming sensation and motor expression. Agency is about being an extension of the environment (i.e., a baby cries, laughs, and uses its body to explore the environment using few, if any, words).

Sensory receptors – cellular levels of reception of incoming sights, sounds, tastes, touches, smells. Sensation is the first stage of Arwood's Neurosemantic Language Learning Theory.

Social competence – having the ability to initiate and maintain healthy social relationships with others.

Social determination – a concept that refers to what we need to know to be able to act like others in our dominant culture.

Social development – levels of understanding of how a person relates to others as an agent. Characterized by stages that reflect the cognitive use of agency as well as the language representative of agency.

Socialization – how a child relates to others by initiating and maintaining relationships.

Social language – language that allows an individual to talk about multiple social relationships among agents, their actions, and their objects.

Social problem solving – a form of critical thinking that requires a concrete level of cognitive development or higher for understanding.

Social skills – acts or behavior that represent what society or the dominant culture expects; rules about social behavior within society or one's community.

Viconic language™ – a term coined by Ellyn Arwood as the process of imposing the characteristics of visual language onto an auditory way of thinking so as to create effective language strategies for someone who thinks in pictures but uses English, an auditory language.

Visual concepts – overlapping visual input that creates mental visual images that are conceptual in nature.

Visual language – thinking in visual ideas; iconic or graphic. Visual language has different properties than auditory languages such as English, French, or German. Examples of visual languages include Mandarin Chinese, American Sign Language, Polynesian, and Hopi.

Visual metacognition – a learner's underlying way of thinking visually that creates mental visual concepts for understanding and developing language.

Visual modality – how material is presented or taught through giving an individual something visual such as a chart or picture in a book to look at.

Visual-motor learning – the shapes of fine-motor movements that store as visual concepts in the visual cortex of the brain, allowing for visual meaning through the overlap of motor patterns.

Visual patterns – visual sensory input that overlaps with other visual sensory input that may form a visual mental image or concept.

Visual perception – the way a learner organizes sensory input from the eyes.

Visual plane – the recognition of points of light by the brain resulting in the formation of horizontal, vertical, and diagonal dimensions (e.g., an individual seeing the consistent shape of points of light resulting in recognition of the shape of an object such as a ball).

Index

A

Agents
  learning to act as, 78
  perception of self as, 48, 85, 86, 102
  See also Preoperational level
American Sign Language (ASL), 42, 164
Antisocial behavior, 98, 99, 125–126
  See also Prosocial behavior
APRICOT I pictures, 45–46, 50, 52–53, 55, 68
APRICOT Learning, Language, and Behavior Clinic, 70
Arwood, E., 8, 14, 21, 164
ASD. *See* Autism spectrum disorders
ASL. *See* American Sign Language
Atresia, 12, 17
Autism spectrum disorders (ASD), individuals with
  drawing by, 152
  imitation not used, 21, 44
  independent functioning, 85, 114, 133, 157, 162, 182
  learning processes, 21–22, 25
  neurological differences, 21, 44
  pattern perception, 44, 45
  preoperational level, 55, 85
  sensori-motor level, 48
  social communication skills, 87
  social development, 96, 98
  visual conceptualization by, 30
  visual perception of shapes, 22

B

Babies
  learning through imitation, 21, 42
  sensory inputs, 42
  See also Sensori-motor level
Behavior
  antisocial, 98, 99, 125–126
  as communication by child, 93, 94
  social stages, 98–99
  See also Prosocial behavior
Behavioral change
  nonverbal methods, 93
  reinforcement, 93
  with Viconic language™, 165
  visuals for, 69, 94, 100–105, 106
Black-on-white visuals, 66–68, 69
Body image development, 94–95
Brain
  mirror neurons, 21
  pattern use, 44
Bubble shapes, 22, 71, 109–111

C

Chinese language, 164
Classrooms
  imitation by students, 157, 167
  positive behavior supports, 60–61
  report cards, 188
  rules, 56–57
  See also Curriculum

Cognitive development levels. *See* Concrete level; Formal level; Preoperational level; Sensori-motor level
Colored visuals, 68
Concept development stage of language acquisition, 16, 23, 66
Concepts
  connecting with language, 29–31, 33, 39
  context of, 65
  developing from patterns, 44, 157
  formal, 158–161, 179–182
  language and, 9, 28–31
  learning meanings of, 14
  learning with visuals, 143–151, 158–161, 162
  perceptual pattern development, 20–22
  visual, 5, 9, 14
Conceptual meaning stages, 23
Concrete level
  academics, 70
  ages of typical development, 56
  behaviors, 90
  case studies, 87–89
  of cognition, 56–60
  of conceptual understanding, 23
  of language, 56–60
  of social development, 98
  visuals used with individuals at, 56–60, 70, 87–89
  writing, 89
Context
  adding to visuals, 165, 168–169
  of concepts, 65
  social, 59–60
  spatial, 168, 169, 173
  in visuals, 54–55, 64, 68
Conventional language, 31, 152n
Curriculum, use of visuals
  benefits for all students, 149
  developing concepts, 153–161
  drawing guideposts, 152
  learning concepts, 143–151, 158–161, 162
  need for, 141–143
  purpose, 143
  selecting, 163–164
  training teachers, 27–28

D

Discrete Trial Training, 74
Drawing in real time, 68, 69, 143, 155
Drawings. *See* Visuals

E

English, as auditory language, 164

F

Finger drumming, 134
Formal level
  academics, 70
  behaviors, 90

case studies, 90–91
  of cognition, 60–61
  of conceptual understanding, 23
  of social development, 98
  visuals used with individuals at, 60–61, 70, 90–91

H

Hand-over-hand (H/H) writing, 38, 47, 71, 82, 83, 101

I

Iconic pictures, 53, 57, 80–82, 166–167
Imitation
  learning through, 21, 42, 157
  not used by individuals with ASD, 21, 44
  of sensory patterns, 43, 157
  by students, 157, 167
Independent functioning, 85, 114, 133, 157, 162, 182

L

Language
  auditory, 164
  clarification of mental concepts, 36
  concepts represented by, 9, 28–31
  conventional, 31, 152n
  meaning provided for visuals, 33–35, 72
  mental dance with visuals, 37–39
  misunderstandings of oral, 141–143
  multiple concepts connected by, 29–31, 33, 39
  performatives, 116–118
  rules, 34–35
  social development and, 97
  symbolic, 60–61
  translation of mental concepts into, 32–33
  visual, 5, 164
Language acquisition
  Neurosemantic Language Learning Theory, 8, 16–18, 21, 65–66
  perception of pictures at stages of, 63–65
  raising overall level, 185–188
  stages, 8, 16–18, 65–66
Language development stage, 16, 23–24, 66
Language functions, for social development, 118, 123
Language levels of visuals
  concrete level, 56–60
  formal level, 60–61
  preoperational level, 48–55
  sensory level, 42–48
Language of Pictures
  drawing pictures, 40
  of individuals, 6
  interpreting pictures, 40
  power of, 140–143
  See also Visuals

AΛPC

Autism Asperger Publishing Co.
P.O. Box 23173
Shawnee Mission, Kansas 66283-0173
www.asperger.net